THE PINK OLEANDERS

THE PINK OLEANDERS

ORGANIC FILM SCENES

ANTI-POETRY COMPOSED BY
STARK HUNTER

WRITTEN AND PRESENTED IN
ANTI-VISION

HOOVER STREET
STUDIOS

proving press

Copyright 2022 by Stark Hunter

Paperback ISBN: 978-1-63337-590-1
E-Book ISBN: 978-1-63337-591-8
LCCN: 2021925518

Published by Mind Tavern Books
Book Design and Production by Columbus Publishing Lab
www.columbuspublishinglab.com

All rights reserved. No part of this book may be reproduced or transmitted in any form or by any means, electronic or mechanical, including photocopying, recording, or by any information storage and retrieval system, without permission in writing from the copyright owners.

Photographs from the Stark Hunter Collection.

INTRODUCTION

ANTIPOETRY IS NOT POETRY. It is writing without rules, standards or restraints. It is stoking the fires of imagination, when the cold facts are absent. It is telling the beautiful human truth, in a universe of cascading fiction. This opus was composed in seven weeks, from March to May, 2021. It was inspired by the mind and work of Gertrude Stein. The production required eight hour days, working in a dark garage. Each chapter is a scene in a mental movie entitled, *The Pink Oleanders*.

Ninety-five percent of the story is true.

The other five percent is based on inference.

This organic film is based on the Letters of Francis Henry Moore (1880-1941). Other information was gleaned from three recorded interviews: Wilfred C. Moore (1969), Geneva Moore (1974) and Shiner Moore (1992).

Thanks to Paul Moore for assistance with dates and other factual details.

The Pink Oleanders is to be realized by the readers inside their own mental theaters— To be seen as: L'art pour l'art.

There are times when music is playing in the film. It is suggested to the reader to find the mentioned title on Youtube and play it as the scene is described.

The Poet thanks you for attending this 'cinéma littéraire.'

STARK HUNTER
MAY 2021

DEDICATED TO THE MOORES
WITH AFFECTION

THE HOUSE ON HOOVER STREET

TABLE OF CONTENTS

PART ONE: "THREE RINGS"

Prologue:	"The Tour"	I
Scene 1:	"Harry's Letter"	1
Scene 2:	"You Showed Me"	5
Scene 3:	"The Wedding"	6
Scene 4:	"The Old Graveyard"	9
Scene 5:	"The Funeral"	11
Scene 6:	"The First Kiss"	15
Scene 7:	"The Visitor"	17
Scene 8:	"The Three Rings"	21
Scene 9:	"That Night In '05"	22
Scene 10:	"Raising The Chandelier"	24
Scene 11:	"A Visitor From Nebraska"	26
Scene 12:	"Anyone For A Hula?"	28
Scene 13:	"Jane Black"	31
Scene 14:	"Yucca Blossoms"	34
Scene 15:	"The Visitor From San Francisco"	37
Scene 16:	"Prayers For The Dying Grandmother"	40
Scene 17:	"No One Saw Us Up There"	43
Scene 18:	"French-Kissing Teresa"	44
Scene 19:	"Suntanning On Top of The Garage"	45
Scene 20:	"I Don't Think She'll Be Alive Much Longer"	48
Scene 21:	"The Devil's Brew"	51
Scene 22:	"The Locket"	56
Scene 23:	"Citizen Harry"	59
Scene 24:	"Hound Dog"	62
Scene 25:	"A Real Hula Sweetheart"	64
Scene 26:	"The Electric Moment"	65
Scene 27:	"Freddie's New Girlfriend"	67

Scene 28:	"Vietnam Is A Terrible Place"	69
Scene 29:	"Hawaiian Music On The 4th"	70
Scene 30:	"Caressing It Like A Football"	73
Scene 31:	"The Shakes"	75
Scene 32:	"The Kiss Inside The Closet"	77
Scene 33:	"Keep It Quiet, Freddie"	80
Scene 34:	"My Grandchild Must Have A Father"	81
Scene 35:	"The Twenty-Third Psalm"	83
Scene 36:	"A Face In The Bedroom Window"	86
Scene 37:	"Kissing In The Water Closet"	87
Scene 38:	"These Cherries Is Ripe"	89
Scene 39:	"Flirting In The Graveyard"	92
Scene 40:	"That Poor Man"	95
Scene 41:	"The Baby Weighed In At 18 Pounds"	97
Scene 42:	"Three Knocks"	99
Scene 43:	"Instead Of Two Guys Wrestling, I See Four"	101
Scene 44:	"Professor Quiz"	104
Scene 45:	"Her Groovy Day-Glo"	106
Scene 46:	"Let Them Dance, Dear"	109
Scene 47:	"Harry Doesn't Look Good"	112
Scene 48:	"Ritz Crackers"	115
Scene 49:	"In The Art Deco Darkness"	118

PART TWO: "THE PINK OLEANDERS"

Scene 50:	"I'm Blind, Ma!"	123
Scene 51:	"Cheese Goulash and French Dressing"	125
Scene 52:	"What Have You Done To Me?"	128
Scene 53:	"Ethel Waters Playing On The Philco"	130
Scene 54:	"Flirting at the Metropole"	132
Scene 55:	"Did She See Anyone?"	135
About the Author		139

PART ONE
"THREE RINGS"

PICTURED IN 1924 ARE HARRY, FREDDIE, SHINER, BABA AND WALT (DINT)

PROLOGUE
"THE TOUR" - APRIL 6, 1968

My pad is on Hoover Street…
I live in the beige house across from the avocado trees.
The lawn in front used to be dichondra grass.
Now it's a mess of different types of grasses.
Not sure how this invasion of unwanted green things happened.
Every year when spring comes,
I get on my knees and pull out each and every weed in the grass.
Same thing for the backyard…

Let's walk down this rocky driveway now…
Here we are.
Look over there.
The winter rains bring tons of high weeds around those orange trees.
Mowing back here is very difficult…
I dread mowing the lawn because it takes forever…
I wish my father would hire a gardener.

This old house was designed by my grandpa, Harry Moore, in 1931.
But I'm sure grandma Baba had something to say about it.
I am positive she put in her two cents as to the final design.
The best part of this place is the basement.
That is where Baba did all the laundry during the 30's, 40's and 50's.
Harry had his secret copper still down there—
Made his own brand of moonshine beer during Prohibition times.
The steps going down there today creak like old car brakes.
The smell always stays the same—musty and dank-like.
The woodwork down there is painted a dark eerie green.
Posted in the open is a notice saying there is poison in the soil.

THE PINK OLEANDERS

I remember when the house was exterminated—
Back in '63, when my parents bought the house from Baba.

That old garage back there looks like it's ready to fall over.
There's a big leak on the roof.
I have often wondered why they designed the garage with a flat roof.
Last winter the hard rains made the leak worse.
Water was pouring into the garage like a waterfall.
Now my dad's cedar chest from the war is completely ruined.
All his old uniforms had to be thrown out.
Back in the '30's, I am sure this garage was in much better shape.
Now look at it.
After we moved in my brother hogged this place.
It was the meeting place for his car club— The Aztecs.
They caroused here all summer back in '63—
All those guys were hot-rodders with ducktails, smoking Marlboros.
They cruised Greenleaf Avenue in their cool hot rods—
Their pony-tailed girlfriends sitting next to them with hickeys.
I can still see those guys in this old garage…
Playing records out here on a hot summer's afternoon—
Dancing with themselves to the music of "Louie, Louie" by the Kingsmen…

There's Baba's bedroom window.
I recall the time when she pounded that glass window like a madwoman.
She was upset with the Aztecs playing basketball back here.
They were making lots of noise as they played.
One time, the basketball landed in her rose bushes by the fence.
So Baba started pounding that cracked window to get them to stop.
But my brother told his friends to keep playing.
I can still see her old shadow behind that window pane—
Trapped inside her steel wheelchair,
Living out the final summer of her life…

STARK HUNTER

I felt bad for Baba.
Everyone, including herself, knew she was dying.
That's why she sold her house to her son, Fred.

That smaller window is the bathroom window.
Come with me inside the house now.
I want to show you Baba's dream bathroom…what we call the Big Bathroom.
We can enter through the back door over there.
Just be careful going up the steps.
This small room was once Harry's den.
Here he smoked his pipe and drank his home brew—
Writing short stories, and numerous letters to family and friends.
He also argued politics here with his neighbor, Mister Cox.
In the Depression years, those two argued long and loud.

Let's go into this next room; it's much larger than the den.
This was my father's bedroom back in the 30's.
His bed was in the corner over there by the black floor vent.
Now it's my room.
Behind that door by the window is a walk-in closet.
All my clothes and magazines are in there.
The other door leads to the hallway.
No doubt Baba loved the color green when they built this place.
The green carpet throughout has been here thirty-seven years.
Still looks like new.

The room across the hall belongs to my parents.
It is the biggest bedroom in the house.
Soon as you walk in there, bam, there's my mother's big mirror.
It spans the entire length of her dressing table.
You can't help but see yourself gawking as you go in there.
Their bed has four tall posts at each corner spiraling up to the ceiling.

THE PINK OLEANDERS

It reminds me of a Queen's bed.
I am sure this was Harry's and Baba's bedroom back in the '30's.
Sometimes I can feel Baba's presence in this room.
One time I smelled roses in here when there were none.
Other times I think I can smell her rose perfume in the evenings…

The next room on the right is Baba's dream bathroom from 1931,
Completely covered on all four walls with black and green tiles.
Step inside and take a look.
Walking into this room is like stepping into a 1930's movie;
The entire floor is covered in black linoleum.
Check out the shower stall with all the shiny, white tiles.
I am sure the mirror behind the sink has seen many staring eyes.
And look how huge the bathtub is; all of this makes me wonder.
What would that white pedestal-sink say if it could talk—
About the souls who have lived in this house down through the years,
Especially the ones who walked this musty hallway in the 30's and 40's—
Especially one relative, on a morning in May in 1941…

This green hallway turns left at the elbow—
The room on the right is my brother's.
I am not allowed to go in there anymore.
One time I found his Playboys hidden under his bed, and he found out.
So now his room is locked up.
No more looking at Playboy centerfolds out behind the garage.

Back in '63 this was Baba's room.
She had a big hospital bed installed next to the southern window.
There was plenty of space left for her steel wheelchair.
I remember Baba spent most of her last days sitting in this room.
Often she would watch the sunset through her open window.
She had her final stroke inside there at summer's end.

I can still hear Baba screaming after she fell on the floor.
This house that night was lit up like it was on fire.
A red and white ambulance arrived silently, and two guys took Baba away.
Never saw her alive again.
Walk into her old room now, you'd still be able to smell Baba's vapo-rub.
It lurks inside the walls and her old closet, like a lost ghost.

Through this door is the service porch.
There's the washer and dryer, both purchased at Sears.
Baba used to get her milk, butter and cream through that small compartment—
Right over there by the back door.
It leads to the outside for the milkman.
That compartment is big enough for three milk bottles.

This is Baba's water closet with a white toilet inside.
Here, let me open the door.
Look up at the ceiling vent.
Can you see all the bougainvillea blooms up there?
That thing is growing crazy on the roof.
Many times I have sat on that toilet in pain—
Feeling terrible from eating something that was spoiled.
But seeing those scarlet bougainvillea blooms through the ceiling vent—
Always brought a calm peace to the gassy proceedings inside here.
Also helping out at times is a copy of the English Book of Common Prayer—
There it is— resting on the toilet tank as it has for the past three decades…

There's my mom's kitchen through this service porch door.
In the 30's this was Baba's dream kitchen.
It is small and old-fashioned but very functional.
Baba's old ironing board is still entombed inside this wall—
Buried there like a stiff mummy from 1963.
My mother spackled over it when we moved in.

This old sink has an odd smell to it.
Bend down here and take a sniff.
What do ya' think?
Yeah. My thought exactly.
Well, it's been thirty-seven years.
What can you expect?

Through this archway is the quaint breakfast room.
This was Baba's favorite room.
Here she served daily meals to her family in the 30's and 40's.
Back then she had lace curtains hanging from these windows,
They looked like big spider webs from England.
Here she drank her daily tea and ate her morning toast.
All these windows in here face east on purpose—

Now this room is used by my mother for typing reports.
She helps my father who has a CPA business in town.
That Underwood typewriter is a permanent part of the decor now.
It reminds me of some weird chattering sculpture.
Those metal trays ascend upward like stacked pancakes.
As you can see, this room is no longer an eating place.
Baba would have another fatal stroke if she could see this room now.

The formal dining room is in there—
Go through this swinging door…
Check out these mirrored door panels that reflect your hands.
The wood paneling is nice in here.
Baba must have spent hundreds of dollars to add all these nice touches.
This is the most haunted of all the rooms here, by far.
I have heard voices seated around this dining table in the night…
Have even heard footsteps coming up the steps from the basement—
When all are asleep…

For years Baba served many a Mackenflap dinner inside this room—
From the spring of 1931 to the autumn of 1957–the time of her first stroke…

Finally, through the archway is the front sitting room.
The fire place over there is the best part of this room.
When the fire logs are lit, it makes this room very warm and cozy.
Another great part of this room is the bay window.
In the mornings the rising sun deposits a new day right through that window.
Baba once said, 'the sun rising would set fire to the pink oleanders out there.'

My mother loves to sit in here and watch the sunrise often.
I am sure Baba did the same back in the 30's.
My Aunt Geneva told me there was once a piano against that wall.
In fact, she would play it all the time—she and her older sister, Viola—
As Harry and the three boys sang tunes by Cole Porter and George M. Cohan.

The fire place has been witness to two weddings—
In 1932 and in 1937.
Both of my uncles said their vows in front of that wooden mantel.
I remember Baba's gray rocking chair was always set against this wall—
Always facing the TV set in the corner, over there by the bay window.
Ed Sullivan was on her TV set every Sunday night back in the 50's.
Baba loved that show more than anything else.
We all saw Elvis sing "Hound Dog" in this room back in '56.
I recall my Aunt Geneva giggled with restrained glee when he sang that song.
Baba, though, didn't like Elvis, and turned her eyes away.
I believe this room is my favorite.
That fire place is in my immediate plans…

SCENE 1
"HARRY'S LETTER" - OCTOBER 9, 1933

Follow me, my friend, down this rocky driveway.
You are in my pulsing time machine now...
Hold on...

Back in '31,
Harry bought bags of granite rock and filled in this middle section.
That must have been some job.
But he had his three strong sons to help him—
Dinty, Shiner, and young Freddie—
A ton of smooth white rocks—
All looking like bird eggs, resting in the California sun.

Can you hear him?
Harry is in his den typing.
Listen to how fast he can type with only his two index fingers.
It's an Underwood from the Salvation Army store in Uptown.
Go inside...
That mug of black hootch on his desk is Harry's homemade beer.
It's his own recipe. Thick as old cough syrup.
That pipe in his mouth is filled with his own brand of homegrown.
Mister Cox thinks it smells like a sick skunk.

Presently he's writing a letter to Missus Mae Morrison.
She's a family friend from Canada, now living in San Francisco.
Harry is quite fond of the Morrison Family—
Especially her beautiful newlywed daughter, Katie Mae—
She being 19 years old, and now, a new mother as well.
It seems Katie Mae is depressed and physically exhausted.

THE PINK OLEANDERS

Harry is now answering Missus Morrison's urgent request for help.
'By all means necessary, have Katie Mae come down here.'
'Yes, and she may stay here absolutely free of charge for as long as she needs.'
'This is the best place for the poor girl to find peace of mind.'
'I insist you send Katie Mae, and I will not accept no for an answer.'

Baba is making a big deal over her little granddaughter, Irene.
Daughter Florence is visiting again.
Her husky husband, George, is working for the fire department.
He never comes by.
Baba feeds and plays with the child as Florence reads Life Magazine.

Now Florence is lying on the living room floor—
Her bare legs suspended in the air…
Propped up like a tableau dancer against Baba's cozy love seat.
Baba asks what is she doing.
Her daughter says she's exercising—
'It's good for the circulation, Mama.'

Harry comes out of his den now with a sealed letter in hand.
He tells Baba to 'stop fussing over that child.'
Baba ignores Harry again as always.
The kettle on the kitchen stove makes its usual whistling sound.
The mailman drops a half dozen letters down the mail chute.
Baba goes into the breakfast room to get them.
Harry says he's writing to Missus Morrison about Katie Mae coming to visit.
Baba says that would be wonderful.
Florence asks if her baby is coming too.
Harry puffs on his pipe and says no—
'Katie Mae needs a break from the baby.'
Freddie comes into the kitchen now, saying he's hungry.
At 16 years old, he resembles Harry in every way—

Eyes, nose, ears, hair color, and body size—
At St. Mary's Church, Freddie is known for his basketball playing.
He is the starting guard for the Newman Club.
Baba tells Freddie to go wash up for lunch.

Freddie turns the bathroom faucets to achieve the perfect temperature.
He stares into the mirror and wonders what David is doing.
David Hilberg is Freddie's closest buddy from Dorland Street.
Together they like to play basketball at the Y, and hang out in the old graveyard.
The afternoon sun is beginning to make its presence known now—
As it filters through the window curtains.
Freddie stares into the mirror and smells grilled cheese sandwiches.

HARRY MOORE SMOKING HIS PIPE—CIRCA 1924

SCENE 2
"YOU SHOWED ME" - DECEMBER 28, 1968

The flickering shadows on these walls look like night demons.
My girl Teresa is sitting close to me on my mother's new sofa.
The stereo console, over there, is playing the Turtles—
"You Showed Me"— on KHJ Boss Radio…
It's near midnight and I'm in love with this 17 year old girl.

We are making out in this darkened room, except,
The fireplace over there is magically aglow,
Like a burning bush of teenage love—
'I love you so much' Teresa whispers into my ear.
Now she smothers my lips with a wet wave of hot moist kisses-
Our ferreting tongues now probe each other's open mouths,
Like slender jets refueling in the high skies…

'Oh Shug Shug, maybe we can go to second base tonight…'
I am shocked to hear this coming from Teresa.
Is she finally giving in to her own strict rule for making out?—
That touching each other in certain areas on our bodies is, well,
Something she decided we both do not necessarily need at this time.
I say to her that I don't think we need to go to second base tonight…
'I agree my love— Not tonight.'
'Let God and all his angels know' she says, 'I'm going to marry you someday.'
'You are my man.'

SCENE 3
"THE WEDDING" - MAY 13, 1937

Hoover Street and its pink oleanders have company today.
All these jalopies and road sedans are awaiting their owners.
They are currently inside the house witnessing a wedding—
In fact, a Catholic wedding without a long Catholic Mass,
With a tall, handsome priest performing the rite—
Father Herman Heidker.
Looks like he's just played a few sets of tennis before coming here.
He and Shiner play tennis often at the Broadway Tennis Courts.

Today's is Shiner's wedding to his pretty bride, Geneva.
Proud parents, Harry and Baba, are standing to the left of their fireplace.
Geneva's grandmother and sister are standing to the right.
Freddie is standing up for Shiner, dressed in a blue suit.
Dinty and Kay stand by the bay window smiling.
Even Mister and Missus Cox are here;
They are standing under the arch by the dining room.
Geneva's maid of honor and oldest sister, Viola, is seated at the piano.
She is suited in lace, wearing a feathered hat.
She is playing "Here Comes The Bride" while reading the sheet music…

Now she steps to the fireplace to stand by her sister…
The ceremony commences with smiles and tears.
Freddie is looking for the ring.
He pretends he can't find it — to scare Baba…

Presently Father Heidker calls for the ring.
It is time for the marriage vows.
Clumsy Freddie now drops the ring next to the piano…

Shiner and Geneva both laugh nervously.
Baba is not amused at all of course.
Freddie bends down to pick it up, and drops it again…
Baba turns beet red and turns her face away…

Harry hugs Baba now as Father Heidker pronounces the couple—
'Man and wife. You can now kiss the bride, Shiner.'
There is modest giggling in the room as Baba hurries into the kitchen.
Harry follows swiftly after congratulating Shiner and Geneva.
Baba is putting finger sandwiches on a large platter.
Harry comes in and hugs her from behind.
He wants to tell her how he feels about Geneva now.
'That boy has found a good one in that girl. I really like her.'
Baba smiles to herself and says nothing…

Harry is bringing up a batch of homemade beer from the basement.
Now Dinty and Freddie are coming up the steps too with more bottles.
Harry says to put all the beer in the breakfast room, out of sight.
Father Heidker is the first to go in there and be served the black brew.

'Harry, your bootleg inspires even the saints in heaven,' he says.
Baba grabs two bottles and takes them to the bride and groom.
'Drink up,' she says discreetly.
'It will be time to bid the devil good morning soon enough.'
Shiner and Geneva now drink Harry's home brew and kiss.
Viola starts playing "Hearts and Flowers" on the piano,
As Florence starts to dance with herself.
Baba now gives her daughter that certain, disapproving look.
'Come on Freddie, dance with me,' Florence says…

Harry is down in the basement with Florence, smoking his pipe.
Florence is smoking also.

Baba does not approve of her daughter smoking.
So Florence is now doing it in secrecy with her father.
She says George works all the time and she needs help with Irene.

'Dad, I can't do this mother thing by myself anymore. It's too hard.'
'I didn't sign up for this solitary confinement thing called marriage.'

Harry tells his daughter to 'buck up girl,'—
Appreciate the fact George even has a job.
'This depression thing is like a monster eating up jobs, girl.'
'Your child needs a working father who can put food on the table.'
'Besides, whose idea was it to elope to Mexico?'
'Your ma still hasn't gotten over that, and neither have I!'

'Sure dad, say all you want about me running away to marry George.'
'I was twenty years old, and pregnant. Who was going to stop me?'
'George is the best thing that's ever happened to me.'
'Now I wonder sometimes.'
'It's true you can't touch a ghost, because it isn't there.'
Now Harry says, 'Here Flo, have a drink. You need it…'

Come stand here, my friend, and look out this dining room window…
Geneva seems sad as she stands with her arm around her grandmother.
There's Shiner tying their two suitcases onto the back of his Model A.
He and Geneva plan to honeymoon in Tombstone, Arizona…
Then swing north to the Grand Canyon.
Shiner is now kissing Baba goodbye.

SCENE 4
"THE OLD GRAVEYARD" - MAY 25, 1964

I am riding in the '63 Impala with my father.
It is Memorial Day and there is no school.
He is smoking a Pall Mall cigarette as we cruise down Broadway.
As we pass Citrus Road, I notice the gates to the old graveyard are open.
Usually Mount Olive Cemetery is locked, and full of trash and weeds.
But the city of Uptown sent in workers last week to clean up the mess.
I ask him if we can go inside to visit the dead today.
He says that would be a nice thing to do.

I ask him if he knows anyone buried at Mount Olive.
He says an old family friend from Canada was buried there—
A young woman named Annie— about thirty years ago.
My father remembers she died of kidney problems after giving birth.
Now he asks me if I'm taking any flowers to Miss Annie.
I tell him yes—three roses from Baba's old rose garden—
Since we know someone is buried there…

This old graveyard is quite beautiful today.
The cleaning crews have turned this weedy dump into something magnificent.
My father says he's never seen it so clean and tidy.
He and his friend David used to play in here as boys back in the 30's.
'This place had a lot of rats and owls back then,' he says…

Now we are walking down the center avenue.
This cemetery is shrouded in shade with dense walnut trees everywhere.
The white tombstones rise up like weird postcards from God…
I am now reading every name and every death date…
I wonder what each dead person looked like while alive.

THE PINK OLEANDERS

I wonder how each person died, and what their voice sounded like.
It is truly like living in a strange dream world— being here today.

My father is quietly following me as I stop and read… stop and read.
The ever-present smell of his Pall Mall cigarette follows me also,
Like some sniffing ghost seeking to get my attention.
The sun is high now and we still have not found Miss Annie's grave…

SCENE 5
"THE FUNERAL" - MAY 17, 1932

This way, my friend.
Today is a sad day.
An old family friend has died and her funeral is this morning.
It will be a brief graveside service over at Mount Olive Cemetery—
Just a stone's throw from Harry's front yard.

Baba is straightening Harry's tie as they dress in their bedroom.
Harry wonders if anyone will be speaking at the service.
Baba suggests he say something.
'Why not you? You've knew her since she was a child.'
'Aren't you one of the pallbearers? Who better?'
Harry says he will write a proper obituary for the North Sydney Herald.
'Her friends back home will want to know.'

Baba stands in front of her full-length closet mirror.
She looks over her dress carefully and turns around to see her backside.
Now she combs her hair into a wavy finish.
Shiner and Freddie walk in, dressed in blue suits.
Freddie asks if his new suit looks copacetic.
Baba laughs and says, 'Copa what?'
Shiner tells Baba he hopes she serves turkey and dressing at the wake.
Baba tells Shiner to hush, and be respectful of the dead…

The sun is rising in the east now;
Its straight rays of white iridescent light are streaking
through the walnut trees—
Like blinding spotlights from heaven.
Harry and Baba are standing by the open grave.

Surrounding them are dozens of elaborate floral wreaths—
Scattered outward in all directions to give people room to come closer.
Harry happily greeted the McClean, Ramsay and Spanks families.
Like Harry and Baba, and Miss Annie too—
They all came to California from Nova Scotia in 1923.

Harry says to his old friend, Purvis Spanks, that it is a sad day.
'Indeed Harry,' says Purvis.' A very tough time for George and the children.'
'Anne was such a sweet lady, and could sing like a bird.'
'Do you remember her singing in the choir back home?'
'Those were wonderful times, especially at Christmas.'
Harry says a collection for George's family should be set up to help them.
Purvis Spanks agrees and says he will talk to the others…

Harry sees the hearse coming down Broadway Street…
It is a black '31 Ford Flower Car with two men inside.
Harry is now joining the other pallbearers by the entrance gate.
Baba looks concerned— she worries Harry may drop the body.
She tells daughter Florence he hasn't been feeling well—
That his asthma is worse because he won't stop smoking.
Florence tells Baba to leave her dad alone. 'Leave him be, Ma.'

The two men now remove Miss Annie's body from the flower car.
Harry and the others take their places around the casket.
Now they are bringing her to the open hole.
The only sound that can be heard is the frail rush of the wind.
The pallbearers place the coffin upon two horizontal boards straddling the hole.

Now a procession of friends is forming under these dark trees…
Family members and the minister are coming this way.
The minister is a protestant, wearing a white collar and black hat.
Now he is standing under a walnut tree with no expression on his face.

Miss Annie's husband, George, gathers his children and cries.
He hugs them with trembling hands and is at a loss for words.
He continues to shake his head in disbelief.

Harry walks up to George now and puts his hand on his shoulder.
He gives him a stuffed white envelope.
A Ford Model A sedan is rumbling down Broadway Street…
It leaves a trail of dust as it passes by.

ANNIE SIMPSON AND HER HUSBAND GEORGE SCOTT—CIRCA 1918

SCENE 6
"THE FIRST KISS" - JULY 16, 1968

Teresa is driving down Hoover Street in her uncle's 68' Camaro.
It is leaving a trail of dust and red blinking lights as it nears Hadley Street.
I am standing in the street in front of my house in a frozen state,
Watching with strong desire, as my new girlfriend turns right.
Only two minutes ago, Teresa and I embraced and kissed for the first time.
I felt her warm wet lips gliding slickly upon mine as we stood here—
Saying goodbye, after spending an hour holding hands on the sofa.
Debussy music was playing on the stereo console when we fell in love.
I am still staring down Hoover Street, hoping for my girl to turn around;
Hoping to feel the pulse of her beating heart again as I take her into my arms...

Just a couple hours ago I took Teresa on a tour of this house.
I took her into the old rooms where Harry and Baba once roamed—
I took her down the basement steps, passing all the canned goods.
I told her about Harry"s moonshine from the '30's, and the poison in the soil.
As we stood down there, Teresa looked at me with romance in her eyes.
I wanted to kiss her, but decided not to.
I felt it was too fast, and too soon.
Instead, she smiled awkwardly, and turned to go back upstairs...

Later, my mother served us a fried chicken dinner in the breakfast room.
It was my mother's friendly repartee during dinner that broke the ice for us.
Next thing I know, Teresa and I are holding hands on the front room sofa—
Listening to "Clair De Lune" on the stereo console...

Presently I'm sitting on the toilet in Baba's old water closet.
This is the place to go if I want privacy.
Now I am looking straight up to the ceiling through the screened air vent.

THE PINK OLEANDERS

I can see the blooms of the bougainvillea up there—
As it grows wild and free atop the beige-colored rooftop.
The odors of smog mixed with roofing tar permeates this little room.
But I can relax and fantasize inside here about Teresa.
I see myself taking her to my bedroom soon and kissing her there.
Then it all comes to an end inside my curious mind—
When I feel the presence of Baba sitting close to me in here.

SCENE 7
"THE VISITOR" - SEPTEMBER 20, 1933

There's Harry stepping out of the water closet.
He's been sneaking deep draws of his special "tobacco" inside there.
Baba has recently told Harry to stop smoking inside the house,
At least while there is company present.
Missus Mae Morrison is visiting from San Francisco.
She plans to stay for a week to relax and visit.
Missus Morrison can't get over how great the house is—
'This is a mansion you have here!'
'It's so roomy, and it has such character!'
'I just love your bathroom! The tile is so beautiful!'
'This breakfast room is just so charming—'
'Perfect for tea time in the morning.'
'I just so love it here.'

Today is beer day down in the basement.
Harry is upbeat as he grabs a bag of potatoes by the back door.
Baba is drinking tea with Missus Morrison in the breakfast room.
The two ladies are laughing over Harry's plans to make beer today.
Harry walks in carrying the potatoes and a bag of baker's yeast.
He smiles and says, 'Time to bid the devil good morning.'

Missus Morrison is coming down the basement steps slowly.
Her petite frame rolls back and forth like an interesting engine.
Now she gazes at all the beer bottles stashed in the crawl spaces.
She asks Harry, 'Just how old is all this beer of yours?'
Harry stands up and says the batch by the stairs is a year old.
He offers to serve her 'a bit of it.'
Missus Morrison says that would be fine, but perhaps after dinner, and a bath.

THE PINK OLEANDERS

She says her goal tonight is to relax in 'that big beautiful bathtub of yours.'
Now she is asking Harry how long it takes to make his own beer.
Harry smiles and says it takes up to six months for his beer to ferment.
'Well,' she says, 'You have quite a set-up down here; very clever indeed.'
Harry says it's easy to make beer. It's the cleaning-up part that's tough.

The rays of an orange sunset are filtering through the bathroom window now.
Missus Morrison is bathing in Baba's big white bathtub.
She is lounging there, admiring still, the tiled design of the bathroom.
Now she hears Harry playing the Philco record player in the dining room.
He puts on "Hearts and Flowers" by pianist, Knuckles O'Tool.
Baba is knocking on the bathroom door—
She's asking if she can rub Missus Morrison's back.
Missus Morrison says, 'That would be just so wonderful.'
Harry sits down now in the dining room and smokes his special tobacco.
On the dining table sit three glasses filled with Harry's year-old batch…

Harry is seated with Baba and Missus Morrison on the front porch.
They are sipping beer while watching the Model A's glide down Hoover Street.
The pink oleanders shake when they pass by the house.
Harry says they're getting faster and more dangerous with each passing day.
Missus Morrison laughs loudly.
She tells Harry the ride from San Francisco was a wild one.
'That Shiner drives his Model A like a crazy boy!'
"He was going 30 miles an hour all the way down the Coast!"
Harry laughs and says 'that Shiner has a lead foot'…
'He loves to torment his Ma by driving fast through Uptown.'
Baba now chimes in, 'He's terrible! Surprised he hasn't been arrested yet.'

Missus Morrison now says her daughter has been sad and quite ill lately.
Times have been difficult since her baby was born.
The marriage with Jim is on the rocks because of too little income.

Katie Mae is welcome to stay as long as she likes.
And if they need some cash to help them get along, that can be arranged too.
Missus Morrison says she will talk to Katie Mae about it later. 'Thanks Harry.'
She puts her hand on his hand as she takes a drink of his beer.
Now Harry asks how she likes his homemade brew.
'I've not had such thick beer before. I just love it, Harry!'

PICTURED IN 1967 IN THE DINING ROOM ARE PAUL, FRED, SHINER AND GENEVA.

SCENE 8
"THE THREE RINGS" - MAY 2, 1961

Come inside, my friend.
I am the 9 year old boy watching TV in the front room...
Don't slam the screen door please.
Even though she isn't here, Baba doesn't like it...

Everyone went to visit Baba at the hospital...
My mom said she had another stroke,
So here I am alone in this big house this morning.
My mom and dad told me to stay in the front room until they come back.
Shiner and Geneva said I could watch their TV,
So I found a dinosaur movie on Channel 9.
This film is okay.
One poor man just got eaten alive by a giant triceratops...

What's that?
I just heard a sound coming from the hallway....
Sounds like someone is walking in there...
I don't dare move beyond the archway...
But I'm scared now, to be honest.
'Who's there?' I say, 'Anyone back there?'
No answer. No sound...
Now the phone is ringing.
This is very strange— It rings three times, then it stops.
Now I am wondering who's calling because everyone is at the hospital.
Maybe it's Uncle Dint calling, or Aunt Flo.
There it goes again...
The phone is ringing like before, and only three times...
Now I am very scared.

SCENE 9
"THAT NIGHT IN '05" - MAY 11, 1935

Harry and Freddie just drove up with a bundle of wood in the trunk.
Today they are making a picket fence in the backyard.
When it's finished, the fence will hide the trash cans that are stored back there.
Baba told Harry she was tired of seeing the trash cans from her window.
'Cover them up for Pete's sake'...
'Build a barrier please or put them behind the garage,' she pleaded.
Harry now is nailing the crisscrossing planks, as Freddie hands him the nails.
Dinty is taking pictures with his new Kodak camera.
'Hey Pa,' he says, as Harry stops hammering and turns around to the camera.
'Say cheese!'

Harry has been telling stories about the old days in Wigan and Blackpool.
Freddie hands his father another nail...
He asks Harry what he remembers most while working on the locomotives.
Harry says that's an easy question to answer—

'That night in '05 at West Leigh'— 'It'd been snowing something fierce'...
'I was firing for Joe Doctor at the time.'
'He was hurt real bad at Hayes' Factory Yard.'
'We were shunting Joe's train when the accident happened.'
'His left leg was crushed bloody.'
'I carried the poor fellow to his home on my back.'
'He never really got over it, and he died a short time later.'
'That was some awful moment in my life. Won't ever forget it.'

Dinty again walks up to them with his ever-ready Kodak.
'Okay brother,' Dinty laughs. "Say cheese!'
Freddie flexes his skinny muscles and says, 'Nail please.'

HARRY CONSTRUCTING THE BACKYARD FENCE IN 1935 WITH HIS SON, FREDDIE, HELPING.

SCENE 10
"RAISING THE CHANDELIER" - JANUARY 21, 1967

'Tape please.'
Uncle Willie is up in the attic right now, and I am with him.
He's installing a new hanging chandelier from the ceiling in the dining room.
This man is 80 years old and he is able to climb up here still.
He is amazing.
This attic is full of thick dust, cobwebs, and electrical wiring.
It reminds me of a big waffle up here with all the crisscrossing two-by-fours.
Uncle Willie says to watch out for the mouse…
Now he is pointing to a sunlit spot in the back of the attic. 'Look.'
Lying on a two-by-four is a dead mouse, caught in an old mouse trap.
Looks like it's been up here for thirty years at least.
All that's left of that mouse is a dusty ball of hair.
The rest of it is long gone.
He says that mouse probably saw its last day when Roosevelt was president.

Uncle Willie is the smartest man I know.
He is my grandfather's brother.
He says when he was my age, he was working in the coal mines.
Now he's retired after working as an electrician for decades in the oil fields.
Whenever a repair is needed around here, especially if it's electrical,
My dad calls on Uncle Wilfred to come to the house and fix it.
And fix it he does…

Now he is raising the chandelier in place…
My mother is delighted with it and thanks Uncle Wilfred.
Uncle Willie says he remembers eating many fine meals at this table years ago.
He claims the best Mackenflap he's ever tasted was served in this room.
And the plum pudding at Christmas time was 'indeed a starry treat.'

My mother is now inviting him to supper.
Uncle Willie says 'Thanks Pauline,'
'But the Missus at home's got something cooking tonight…'

Now my father is backing the white Impala out of the driveway.
Uncle Willie waves goodbye from the front seat.
The car pulls away with my father smoking a Pall Mall cigarette.
I now ask my mother what's for supper tonight.
She says chicken and dumplings with green beans.
I say nothing because I really don't like chicken and dumplings.
I'd rather have Mackenflap, whatever that is…

SCENE 11
"A VISITOR FROM NEBRASKA" - DECEMBER 25, 1934

The house is smelling like cooked bacon.
There is nothing like that homey smell, especially today.
There's Freddie opening presents under the Christmas tree.
Baba is sitting on her sofa looking sad.
Harry is not home this morning.
He is at the oil fields today working a 6 hour shift.
Shiner is sitting on the green carpet telling Freddie to 'slow down.'
Freddie laughs because he is going slow in opening his presents— on purpose.
He is trying to torment Shiner and his Ma.
Baba smiles at Freddie because she knows he's playing his games again—
That is— trying to annoy and get a rise out of her.
Baba decides to sit silently as usual and pretend not to be bothered…

Freddie now can't decide which present to open next.
He asks Shiner if he has a coin.
Shiner says he has a coin in the Model A— a dime.
Baba can no longer stand this nonsense, and says to forget it.
She tells Freddie to open the one with the green ribbon next—
And to 'make it right quick.'
'Okay, Ma,' he says laughing. 'Right quick.'
Now he asks Shiner if the dime in his car is a Mercury head…

It is Christmas evening and Harry is home from work.
Baba is beaming as she walks into the dining room carrying her plum pudding.
Now she pours a shot of rum over the top and lights a match…
Harry says, 'Merry Christmas everyone. Isn't that a pretty sight.'
Now the family is clinking their glasses for a slice of Baba's magic.

George and Flo are here with little Irene…
Harry's brother, Willie, is here with his wife, Annie, and their boy, Bert.
Dinty and Kay are seated at the table talking with Shiner and his new friend—
A sweet gal from Nebraska— named Geneva.
Shiner tells Dinty they met at the bank two weeks ago.
'I was working, and then this beautiful girl walked up to my window.'
Shiner says she's as sweet as ice cream.
'Just come to California this month.'
Baba thinks Shiner ought to slow down with the 'Nebraska girl.'
Shiner thinks his Ma ought to stand by him for the happy days to come…
'How does love slow down, Ma?'

SCENE 12
"ANYONE FOR A HULA?" - APRIL 18, 1953

Saturday chores are occurring behind the house.
There's Shiner and Geneva putting in a new sidewalk by the garage.
The old one was put in by Harry back in 1935.
But now, because of drainage problems, a new sidewalk is needed.
Shiner has an old Victrola playing inside the garage—
Hawaiian pedal steel.
Baba is sunbathing on the backyard lawn.
She now tells Shiner to turn up the music, 'Will ya?'
'Hey Gene,' Baba says laughing, 'Anyone for a hula?'
Now Geneva is dancing her own version of the Hawaiian hula…
She comes to Baba and invites her to get up and join her…
Now both ladies are dancing on the dichondra carpet of grass—
With Sol Hoopii himself playing his pedal steel,
Sounding like an exotic jungle bird…

Here come Fred and Pauline with their two sons…
Walking slowly down the rock-strewn driveway—
They have come to visit grandma Baba on this warm spring afternoon.
Paul is the oldest boy at age six.
Mike is the youngest at age one.

Baba stops dancing and tells Geneva to go get her camera.
'Time to take pictures!' Baba says happily…
Now Geneva is standing in the sun.
She has Baba's Kodak camera and snaps two pictures of the young family—
One with Baba in it, and one without.

Harry says the sidewalk is finished and that it needs to dry now.

Pauline tells little Paul not to get close to the wet cement.
'Oh, it's okay,' Baba says. 'Let him run around for Pete's sake.'
Now Uncle Shiner stares at his Ma with a stern look.

Aunt Geneva suggests Baba sign her name in the cement before it drys.
Baba likes the idea, and now goes to her orange tree to find a stick.
She finds one on the ground about six inches long.
Baba says she will now sign her real name— Phoebe, in the drying cement.
All are standing on the dichondra lawn, watching.

Geneva says Baba ought to also write the year "1953" to mark the occasion.
Uncle Shiner looks like he is fit to be tied…
He and Geneva now walk into the back den to have a private chat.
The old screen door, once used by Harry a decade ago, slams loudly…

'There,' Baba says proudly upon finishing the task. 'For posterity.'
Now Baba says the music is not playing. 'Hey Shiner, what happened?'
But he and Geneva are not outside anymore.
'Sing to us, Ma,' Fred says, as his two sons walk to the wet cement…
Now Baba sings without music—

"There'll always be an England
And England shall be free
If England means as much to you
As England means to me…'

AUNT GENEVA IS LIGHTING THE CHRISTMAS PLUM PUDDING IN THE DINING ROOM, 1964. HER NEPHEWS, PAUL AND MIKE, LOOK ON. THE WOODEN SWINGING DOOR TO THE KITCHEN IS OPEN. THE DOOR TO THE HALLWAY IS AT RIGHT.

SCENE 13
"JANE BLACK" - JUNE 4, 1937

My friend!
Can you hear them?
Let us amble down this driveway again so you can hear them better…

Harry is talking politics with Mister Cox inside the den.
We don't need to go inside and disturb their conversation.
We can hear them fine from these descending basement steps…

Mister Cox is a partially bald man wearing white suspenders.
He is Harry's best friend and a loyal next door neighbor.
Harry is saying it is ridiculous for school kids to be saluting the American flag.
Mister Cox smiles and takes a drink of Harry's home brew…
He says the school kids need to learn about loyalty to their country.
'What better way…?'

Harry draws on his pipe, 'You Americans are just crazy for all the flag stuff.'
'This is the rankest, most militaristic country in the entire world!'
Baba walks in now and offers both men a tray of crackers and cheeses.
Mister Cox says thanks, and tells Harry he is right about America's big stick.'
Harry laughs loudly at the remark, and begins to cough deeply from his lungs.
Baba stands by Harry and shakes her head as his coughing attack continues…
'You're smoking too much, Pa,' she says, 'your lungs sound bad.'

Now Mister Cox is reading Harry's newest short story, entitled "Jane Black."
Baba says the story 'is a bit good in parts, but drags a wee bit too.'
Harry tells Baba he worked hard on it and wants to send it to publishers.
Mister Cox says he likes the story, 'but what about the three rings?'
Harry says Mister Cox needs to keep reading to find out…

Now Mister Cox has finished the story.
'So it was Miles Stanton who rang the doorbell.'
'Poor, confused Jane,' he says. 'At least it was a happy ending for her.'
He thinks Harry ought to change the title to "Three Rings."
Harry says he appreciates the suggestion, and draws again from his pipe…

Mister Cox now watches Baba walk out of the den.
He waits and then asks Harry if he's heard from Missus Morrison.
Harry says it's been three years since he's heard from her.
'Not sure what happened. I wrote her but there was no return letter…'
Mister Cox says Missus Morrison was a good poker player.
Harry says he misses her deeply, and thinks of her often.
'She always played with a full deck, my friend, in every way imaginable.'
Mister Cox laughs and takes another swig of Harry's black beer.

It is twilight time now and Geneva walks into the den looking for Harry.
He is seated in his chair smoking his pipe and drinking his beer.
Geneva says dinner is now being served in the breakfast room.
Harry says he'll be in 'pronto —that's Spanish for real quick.'
Geneva reminds him the food will get cold if he doesn't go eat.
Harry smiles and says, 'Don't know what I'd do without me beer and me pipe.'

PAULINE WILLIAMS — CIRCA 1942

SCENE 14
"YUCCA BLOSSOMS" - DECEMBER 21, 1968

Teresa and I are in the den now, hiding from the rest…
The family Christmas party is taking place, and the old house is full of relatives.
Teresa looks good tonight in her new outfit— a plaid skirt with matching vest.
Her dark panty hose makes her Mexican legs look even more alluring.
She is wearing her church-black shoes that have been shined.
Tied to her long black hair is a white ribbon, which I am tugging on now.
'Ouch,' Teresa yelps, 'That hurts. Why are you pulling on my hair ribbon?'
I smile and tell her, 'I want to kiss you now.'
Teresa likes the idea, and now we embrace—
Our moist lips touching and sliding like mad worms.
She hurriedly inserts her warm tongue through my puckering lips…

Now Aunt Geneva walks in. 'Oh! Pardon me. Thought no one was in here.'
'It's okay Gene,' I say embarrassed, as Teresa and I separate ourselves.
She says we're a cute couple, and asks how long we've been going together.
Teresa looks at me and answers shyly: 'Mike's been my boyfriend since summer.'
'Oh how wonderful!' Aunt Geneva says, while winking at me.
Now she reminds us dinner is being served in the breakfast room.
'Mikey, your mother is such a sweet dear. So much wonderful food in there!'
'Merry Christmas!'

Now we are walking through the hallway to the dining room.
I can hear the voices of Uncle Shiner, Aunt Flo and my mother dominating.
On our right, I notice my brother's bedroom door is open.
He came home a couple days ago from Redding with the Hong Kong Flu.
He told my parents his temperature had been up to 104.
Now with my mother nursing him, his temperature has decreased.
He has a glass jar on his bedside table, full of his green coughed-up spit.

Teresa sticks her head inside and says, 'Hi Paul. Hope you're feeling better.'
Paul says thanks, and asks if we could close his door for him.

As we walk into the dining room I notice there are relatives everywhere…
I wonder who is here tonight…
There's Uncle Dint and Aunt Kay sitting by the bay window in the front room.
Their two daughters, Marilyn and Susie, are sitting by the fire place.
Their husbands, Warner and Bill, stand by them—
Big glasses of my mother's Yucca Blossoms sit cradled in their hands…
Aunt Flo and her husband George are seated on the sofa.
Their daughter Irene, and her family, are sitting around the dining room table.
Uncle Willie and Aunt Annie are here also. They are in line for dinner…

Now my mother is playing a Wayne Newton Christmas album on the console.
Aunt Geneva says she just loves that singer. 'What's his name again?'
Now my mother ignores Aunt Geneva's question and rushes into the kitchen.
Uncle Shiner is talking to my father in the breakfast room as they dish up.
'Hey Fred, heard about your Impala exploding. How did that happen?'
My father explains the car stalled, became flooded, then caught fire.
'Mikey was driving a bunch of kids from a football game.'

It is later in the night now…
Teresa and I are hiding back here in the den again.
Some of the kids and adults out there are coughing too much,
So we decided to break away…
We are kissing deeply as we sit close together on the rattan love seat.
Teresa has one of her legs on my lap as she french-kisses me repeatedly…
Now I have my hand on her opened right thigh.
I like the feel of her pantyhose on my curious exploring fingers…
I put my lips to her ear, and ask if we could go to second base tonight.
 'Shug,' she says, 'That would be wonderful… but…'
'But what, my love?' I ask, as I continue to bathe Teresa's neck in wet kisses.

'It's just…ooh I love your kisses… I don't think our relationship needs that.'
Now Teresa winks at me and says there's an old saying in life—
'If it's worth having, it's worth waiting for.'
I get up now and put on a new record— The Turtles' "You Showed Me."
Teresa gets up from the love seat, and now, we are dancing cheek to cheek…
Aunt Geneva comes in and says, 'Oh, pardon me. I didn't know you two…'
'No problem Gene,' I say, as Teresa looks at me with eyes that say, 'Her again?'
Geneva says the plum pudding is being set aflame in the dining room now—
'Hurry Mikey, you'll miss it!'
Teresa and I go into the dining room to see the lighting of the plum pudding—
This time, prepared perfectly by Baba's student, my mother.
With a glass of rum, she pours the brew over the pudding and lights a match.
'Pauline,' says Aunt Kay, 'That is so beautiful!'
All the relatives gasp as the flame lights up the darkened room.
I take Teresa's hand into mine now. I will never forget this moment…

SCENE 15
"THE VISITOR FROM SAN FRANCISCO" - OCTOBER 31, 1933

Missus Katie Mae Clancy is folding the laundry down in the basement.
She is the former Katie Mae Morrison—
Presently visiting for two weeks from San Francisco…
Harry is cleaning his copper still after cooking a new batch of beer.
He says to Katie Mae that the laundry is Phoebe's job.
He now insists she stop working like 'someone's hired girl, and relax.'

Harry gets up from his stool now and takes the clothes from Katie Mae.
'Sit down Katie Mae,' he says smiling. 'You've come here to relax, so relax.'
'Indeed, what would your mother say if she saw you working for us?'
Katie Mae relents and sits on the stairs which ascend to the hallway…

She says it will be fun tonight to give out the candy to the children.
Harry lights his pipe now and says the costumes are really something to see.
'I saw some kids last year coming by as clowns and devils from hell'…
'You have to answer to them or else. Phoebe hates to open the door to 'em.'
Katie Mae says she'll give out the candy tonight if that's fine with him.
Harry thanks Katie Mae for volunteering at the door tonight.

Now Harry asks if she misses her baby.
Katie Mae says she misses her son terribly, and she is sad she can't see him.
Harry says he understands how she must feel being separated.
'It can't be easy living life in ill health and exhaustion as you have,' he says.
Katie Mae now grabs Harry's arm and holds it with gratitude.
She begins to weep in Harry's arms as he now holds her closely to his chest.
'It's okay my dear…' he says in a whisper.
Now she tells him she's been so lonely without Jim and the baby.
She says she's homesick, and can't stand being away from them any longer…

Now Missus Clancy whispers to Harry words no one can hear—
—That it's okay to visit with her at night time— when all are asleep…
'I often cry late at night,' she says. 'It's the worst time for me.'
Harry says he works late in his den at night—
But would be happy to sit with her if she needs some company…
'Just knock three times,' Harry whispers, 'and I'll know it's you…'
'Thank you. Harry. Three knocks.'

HARRY'S THREE SONS: SHINER, FREDDIE, AND DINT - TAKEN IN THE LATE 30'S.

SCENE 16
"PRAYERS FOR THE DYING GRANDMOTHER" - SEPTEMBER 15, 1963

Baba is sitting in her steel wheelchair.
She is sad as she stares out her dining room window.
The world outside today looks smoggy and hot…
In her boney hands I can see a black-beaded rosary.
I think she is praying…

My mother has just bathed Baba in the big bathroom.
Baba has been crying loudly about all her pains…
My mother just keeps doing what's she's been doing, saying.
'I know Phoebe.'
Everyday I see my mother taking care of my sick grandmother—
She bathes her, feeds her, wipes her—
And pushes her around the house in the steel wheelchair.
Lately my mother has been saying to my father that she's getting tired of it…

Now Baba says she wishes for 'a priece of toast and a crup of tea.'
I am sitting on the front room couch and I can see my mother in the kitchen…
She's giving Baba a dirty look as she puts two pieces of bread into the toaster.

Today is Sunday, so my parents are going to Mass to pray for Baba.
Kathy, the registered nurse who visits Baba, is here today.
She has her black hair up in a big beehive, and can speak Italian.
She has a very large chest like my mother's—
My father likes large chests…

Now he's putting a 5 dollar bill into the offering envelope.
He is dressed in his brown catholic suit with black shoes.
My mother is wearing her new blue dress with white hat and gloves.

I am wearing my usual catholic school clothes…
They probably need to be washed soon.
There is a yellow ring around the collar from sweating at school.

My father is driving the '63 Impala up Broadway now…
The radio is on KRLA with Sunny and the Sunglows singing "Talk To Me."
My mother is smoking a Salem menthol.
She says Baba is driving her crazy with her constant griping.
'If she says 'a priece of bread and a crup of tea one more time, I swear…'
Now my father lights a Pall Mall and fills the Impala with white smoke.
'She's dying Pauline,' he says.'Good God. Have some patience.'

There's St. Mary's up ahead…
I can see dozens of catholics standing at the church entrance.
The women are wearing scarves and hats on their heads.
Their children are holding missals and scapulars.
The fathers are dressed in suits as they carry crying infants.
My father is having trouble finding a parking place…
This parking lot is filled with dozens of cars of every make and model—
My mother now sees a spot over by the nun's convent gate.
My father drives over and parks, as my mother puts on red lipstick.
She is looking at herself in the rear-view mirror…

GENEVA, BABA AND AUNT ANNIE GOING OUT ON THE TOWN— 1940'S

SCENE 17
"NO ONE SAW US UP THERE" - JUNE 9, 1955

Aunt Geneva has just come inside the house.
She has been suntanning in her bathing suit on top of the garage.

Up there one can see all the way out to downtown Los Angeles—
Sixteen miles of wadded-up human lives—all leading to City Hall.
My mother told me she and Geneva used to suntan in the nude up there—
Back in 1944— when the guys were away to war.
I remember it bothered me when she told me that.
'Don't worry Mikey,' she said. 'No one saw us up there.'

Aunt Geneva says it's time for a shower as Baba walks by in the hallway.
'Hurry up, dear,' Baba says, 'Dinner will be ready soon.'
'Thank you, Phoebe. I'll hurry.'
Aunt Geneva spends 20 minutes in the shower…

I am the little 3 year-old boy who is now barging into the closed bathroom…
He sees Aunt Geneva naked and surprises her.
She grabs a towel and says, 'Hi Mikey. What are you doing in here?'
The little boy finds his attractive, undressed aunt to be strangely appealing.
Aunt Geneva continues to towel off her wet body…
Now the little boy asks his aunt to show him her naked chest.
Aunt Geneva laughs abruptly and says, 'Mikey!
What are you asking me, dear?'
'I want ta see your chest,' I repeat.
Now with a nervous giggle, Aunt Geneva reveals her flat chest to the boy.
The little boy smiles widely, and runs out of the bathroom…

SCENE 18
"FRENCH-KISSING TERESA" - JANUARY 11, 1969

Teresa and I are french-kissing like horny newlyweds on the front room couch.
The room is dark except for the flickering glow of the fireplace.
The shadows on the walls dance like creepy ghosts—
Peeping on us teenagers making innocent first-base love…

There has been a 17th birthday party this evening for me.
The bright-colored streamers still hang on the ceiling—
Like dry lifeless vines in a day-glo jungle.
Teresa gave me a poetry book by Rod McKuen called Lonesome Cities.
We had cake, ice cream, pizza, and Teresa played Marvin Gaye on the console.
Now everyone has left and we are alone…

Teresa is presently kissing and sucking on my neck like a vacuum cleaner.
'Oh Mike,' she says, as she lies down on her back. 'I just love you so much.'
'I love you too, Goobe, You are so beautiful—
Do you think we can go to second base now?'
'Shug,' she says, as she kisses the inside of my ear—
'I want so much to express to you how much I love and adore you!'
'But,…' I respond, knowing what she'll be saying next…
'But… I truly feel our relationship does not need that right now—
— Our love is too strong and too special for that stuff. Don't you think?'
'Sure,' I say with mild confusion. 'Who needs it?'
Now Teresa opens up her legs, and brings me down to lie on top of her…
'Now now now,' she reminds me, as I start to get excited. 'That will do.'
Now I remember how James Bond succeeded with all those babes…
'He used his gun,' I thought.

SCENE 19
"SUNTANNING ON TOP OF THE GARAGE" - JUNE 1, 1935

Freddie is hiding behind a massive white tombstone at Mt. Olive Cemetery.
His friend David is presently running through the weeds and the debris—
Looking behind trees and other massive tombstones for his elusive buddy.
Now Freddie makes ghostly, booing sounds to scare David into running away…
'Not today Fred,' David Hilberg says. 'Only your scrawny muscles scare me…'

Now Freddie points to the grave of Miss Annie.
He says his dad once knew her back in Canada when she was small.
'She had a bunch of kids when she died,' Freddie says.'That last one killed her.'
David says having babies is man's work, not a woman's.
'Why, Freddie,' he laughs, pointing now at his friend's belly—
'I do believe I see a little pig inside there! Look at that gut!'

Freddie says David ought to come over to his house today.
He says it's Saturday, and that means Shiner's pretty girlfriend is visiting again.
Freddie says her name is Geneva, and she likes to suntan on top of the garage.
'Come on,' says Freddie. 'We can see her from the bathroom window…'

Now Freddie and David are walking up Hoover Street hurriedly…
The pink oleanders are in full bloom now, and are casting benign shadows.
They see Geneva's car parked in the driveway… a Ford 3 Window Coupe—
They enter into the house and check to see if anyone is home.
Freddie says it looks like his parents and brother have gone out.
'All are out…except Geneva…'

Freddie leads David into the big bathroom.
He steps in front of the sink and flexes his muscles into the mirror.
'I'm scared,' says David, while sizing Freddie's muscles with two fingers.

Now Freddie goes over to the window, parts Baba's curtain, and looks outside…
He says, 'Dave, come here!'
Freddie points to the garage and says, 'That's Geneva Engelhart's head.'
'She's up there right now with only a bathing suit on. Can you imagine?'
'I can't imagine, Freddie,' says David Hilberg. 'I'm so glad I'm not blind…'

Minutes of staring and wondering have passed by…
Freddie and David are still behind the bathroom window waiting…
But now they hear the front door opening.
Freddie says they need to go down to the basement.
They hear the voices of Harry, Baba and Shiner talking about Geneva.
Harry says, 'Anyone home?'

Freddie and David now exit the basement through the outside door…
They are ascending the outside steps as quietly as they can…
Baba comes to the den screen door and says, 'We're back, Gene!'
Now the boys see Geneva Engelhart standing up…

Geneva climbs down the wooden ladder attached to the side of the garage.
She is wearing a sun dress and a yellow bonnet.
She sees Freddie and David now.
'Hi Freddie,' she says, looking a little embarrassed. 'Who's your friend?'
'This is David. He's blind…'

FREDDIE IN 1931, AGE 14

SCENE 20
"I DON'T THINK SHE'LL BE ALIVE MUCH LONGER"" - JANUARY 14, 1962

You and I are riding in the '58 Impala right now…
We're riding down Broadway to Hoover Street, passing the old graveyard…
KRLA is playing the "Peppermint Twist" by Joey Dee on the radio…

My father is parking the Impala in front of Baba's house.
My brother Paul is sitting in the front seat wearing his white jacket.
Today we are visiting Baba who is bedridden inside her room.
For the past two years she has had recurring strokes…

Usually we go inside through the back door into the service porch.
But today the back door is locked.
So now my father says we need to try the doorbell up front…

Finally the front door is opening, but this time,
It isn't Uncle Shiner or Aunt Geneva answering.
It's Kathy, Baba's live-in nurse.
'Hi Fred,' she says happily. 'Hi boys. Come to visit your grandma?'
Paul says nothing, but I say yes…

Kathy is wearing her tight-fitting nurse outfit—
Showing her big chest, and a white caduceus pin on her lapel.
My father asks Kathy if Shiner and Gene are out.
Kathy says they went to church at St. Mary's for the high noon mass.
She says they may go get lunch afterwards at the Beverly Fountain.
'How's my mother doing today?' my father asks.
Kathy smiles and says Baba is stable—
Which is 'good considering all those strokes she's had.'
Now my father says he needs to talk to her for a few minutes…

'Certainly Fred,' Kathy says, as she follows him down to the basement.

Presently Paul and I are visiting Baba inside her bedroom…
She is happy to see us as she lies in a steel hospital bed.
Her stainless steel bedpan lies on the floor under her steel wheelchair.
Poor Baba. She looks pale and very weak.
Paul asks if she's been feeling better lately.
Baba can barely talk, but manages to shake her head yes.
Now she looks up at us and smiles. She slurs her words—
'Doing better now, but this morning… I was feeling real bad.'
I can tell Paul is feeling uneasy because Baba can't talk much.

Now I notice my dad's been gone for awhile…
He said he needed to talk to Kathy about Baba.
But it's been at least fifteen minutes, and Baba is getting tired…

Finally I can hear them walking up the basement steps…
Kathy is laughing at something my dad said to her.
Now Kathy says she needs Baba to endorse her paycheck.
'Not a problem,' my dad says. 'I will sign it over for her.'
It was sad seeing Baba today.
I don't think she will be alive much longer…

FRED, MIKEY, BABA AND PAUL, TAKEN IN 1962 IN BABA'S ROOM

SCENE 21
"THE DEVIL'S BREW""" - NOVEMBER 22, 1931

Harry is presently sitting on the toilet inside the water closet…
He is sneaking deep draws from his pipe before Baba finishes her shower.
She has let it known that pipe smoking is not allowed inside their new house.
Tomorrow is Harry's fifty-first birthday,
So Baba is having a family party today, since it is Sunday.
Harry draws in his special tobacco a half dozen times before she finishes…

Now the shower has been shut off in the big bathroom.
Baba is toweling off as she stares into her new mirror….
She shakes her head now, thinking her goiter is getting worse.
Baba secretly worries about it, as she worries about Harry's bad lungs.
She needs to hurry now if she expects to get to Noon Mass on time…

Now she hears voices coming from the back yard.
Baba parts the window curtain to see who's outside.
Sitting in lounge chairs atop the garage are Shiner, Dinty and his wife Kay.
Baba hopes the garage will hold up, what with so many bodies up there.
Freddie is dribbling a basketball, and spots his Ma looking out the window.
He stops and waves to her.
Baba is embarrassed and quickly closes the curtain…

It is quarter past noon.
Harry is in his den arguing with Mister Cox about prohibition…
Harry says the entire system in America has been a complete fiasco.
Mister Cox says he agrees with President Hoover's assertion—
That the Prohibition is indeed a noble experiment—
'It is much needed to save American families.'
Harry laughs and now offers Mister Cox a bottle of his 'six-month' brew…

THE PINK OLEANDERS

He says the liquor laws are stupid here—
'That every body and his brother is making their own beer'…
'It's cheaper and better tasting,' says Harry.
Mister Cox now raises his beer bottle to Harry—
'Here's to your bank account, my birthday friend!'

Now it is half past noon…
Purvis Spanks has arrived, and the entire Scott Family as well…
Harry greets Purvis with a firm handshake and a brotherly hug.
Purvis asks, 'Where's Phoebe?'
Harry says she's at Noon Mass, 'praying for my condemned soul no doubt.'
'My friend,' says Harry. 'How do you like our new digs?'
Purvis can't believe his eyes at how big and cozy it is…
'Like a mansion, Harry!'

George Scott and his pregnant wife are telling their four children to behave—
To go into the backyard and play, but to stay off the garage roof…
Harry hugs Annie Scott and says he recalls when she was just a 'little thing.'
'Now look at you,' he exclaims. 'Expecting another child! How wonderful!'
George Scott discreetly asks if Harry has any of the 'Devil's Brew' on hand…
Harry laughs and proposes a rendezvous in 'hell' for 'special refreshments.'
He looks at Annie and says she is invited too for 'spirits on this special day.'
Annie says 'thank you,' but her doctor would not approve.
'Well,' says Harry, with a wink in his eye—
'Come down to the basement if you change your mind…'

It is now three-quarters past noon…
While the men are downstairs in the basement,
Their wives sit in the front sitting room on Baba's pleated sofa.
Flo is playing on the new upright piano— "Just One More Chance."
Freddie joins her now, and is singing the popular lyrics like Bing Crosby…

*"I've nothing to hide,
I'd bury my bride for,
Mmmm bo ba baboo baboo bo baboo…"*

The visiting ladies are laughing now at the entertaining fourteen year-old boy…
Flo stops playing now and tells Freddie to 'stop singing like that.'
'Freddie,' she says, 'You are the worst singer since Lady Florence Foster!'
'Okay Lady Florence,' Freddie says, 'Try singing it yourself then!'

Meanwhile, Harry is downstairs sharing his 'best beer' with his friends…
Purvis Spanks and his wife are enjoying a beer, as well as George Scott.
Even Harry's old friend, Andrew Ramsey, is down here, drinking the hootch…
Now Annie Scott is carefully coming down the basement steps…
She's holding her distended stomach as she joins her husband, George.
'Join us Miss Annie,' says a delighted Harry. 'I have plenty to go round.'

It is now one o'clock…
The new Hoover Street house is filled with family and friends—
Flo is still playing the piano for everyone…
The back yard, too, is crowded with children playing, and adults smoking…

Harry remains in his basement with Purvis, George and Andrew.
They are discussing the employment situation in Southern California.
Harry says he's lucky to have had consistent work here, since landing in 1923.
But he can't say the same for most working men in this area…
'And what's worse,' Harry says, 'living here is a regular hold-up—
'Butcher's fees, taxes, and doctor's bills… there's no end to it.'
Harry says he bets all those old Sydney Miners back home are thinking—
'California is the land of sunshine and the easy life!—
Well tell 'em otherwise!'

Harry says he has to work the night shift tonight, which isn't so bad.

'It's a job… puts bread on the table'…
'And it built this fine house by scrimping every damned dime!'

Now Missus Ramsey is calling down from upstairs, asking for George Scott.
She says his wife is sick in the bathroom. 'She's vomiting, George.'
George rises instantly and hurries up the stairs to the hallway.
Inside the big bathroom is Annie Scott, kneeling before Baba's new toilet.
George asks if she is okay, and if she needs his help…
Annie says she got it all out, and feels better already…

Harry has now stepped in to check on the pregnant woman.
'My drink too much for ya, Miss Annie?' he asks.
'Perhaps you've had enough of the recipe for one day.'
Now Harry gives George Scott a reassuring wink…
'I suppose, sir, you have bid the devil good afternoon on this fine day.'

It is now quarter past one o'clock…
Baba now comes into the house, returning from Mass with Shiner…
She finds her new home filled with family, and Harry's friends…
'Thank you all for coming today,' Baba says happily.
'Time for sandwiches!'

THE MOORE HOUSE ON HOOVER STREET— CIRCA; 1933.
HARRY IS PICTURED TO THE LEFT ON THE FRONT PORCH.

SCENE 22
"THE LOCKET" - MAY 2, 1956

The four-year-old boy in Baba's arms is looking at something special…
They are in Baba's bedroom, standing by her tall dresser.

She is delighted that her youngest grandchild is here today.
Though Baba has had problems with her thyroid, she is feeling well.
Babysitting her grandchildren is still a special treat for her…
'As long as my heart can stand it,' she says.
Now her young grandson is going on a tour of her beautiful big house…

Baba is showing the boy a locket pin given to her by Freddie during the war.
He recognizes it as a little house with a red chimney, and an American flag—
Waving in the wind on top of the slanted roof.
It is just like Baba's house.
Closed inside, behind a little door, is a tiny photograph of Baba hugging Fred.

Baba says his daddy is hidden inside the locket—'Where is he, Mikey?'
Now Baba opens the little door and says, 'there he is!'
'See your dad,' she says to the boy. 'He's leaving for war in his uniform.'
The boy takes the pin into his hands…
He is amazed at how small the photograph is—
And how it still fits inside Baba's little lapel pin…

Now Baba is leading the boy down the basement steps…
'Be careful Mikey.'
The boy smells something old and musty in the air.
As he walks down the steps he sees dozens of canned goods in the crawl spaces.
There are peaches, pears, creamed corn, peas and green beans galore.
Baba is pointing to them all as she leads the boy to the bottom step…

'It's cool down here in the summers,' she says to the boy.
'Some times when I'm sad and miss your grandpa, this is where I come.'
'This basement was where he liked to be…making his special beer…'
'Today,' she says, 'is a sad day for grandma Baba…'

The boy looks around and sees boxes, and wet clothes hanging on a line…
In the far corner is a Bendix washing machine.
Baba says it is time to go upstairs now— that's it's almost time for lunch…

Now Baba is taking the boy down the hallway past the big bathroom…
Past the guest room that was once the room Baba shared with Harry—
Now she turns left into Uncle Shiner's and Aunt Geneva's bedroom…
She points to the painting on the wall of an enchanted land in the orient…
'A land far away,' she says to the boy—
'Where life is always good, and hearts never break…'

Now Baba takes the little boy into the far back room—
'This was his den,' she says…
'Your grandpa loved it back here— before you were born…'
'Sometimes I think I can hear him still— pounding on that typewriter of his…'

Baba now looks through the screen door…
She hears footsteps inside her sad, remembering mind…
Now she thinks she sees him —
Walking up the basement steps as he did so often—
Her tough-skinned gentleman from the English village of Aspull—
Emerging full of life into the sunshine of another day, ready to go to work…
'Harry,' she whispers to herself, 'Is that you?'…

BABA IN FRONT OF HER NEW CAR— CIRCA: 1925

SCENE 23
"CITIZEN HARRY" - AUGUST 15, 1938

Harry is walking up the outside basement steps on this summer morning…
He is heading to the garage, carrying his lunch and a tool box…
Baba is in the den, telling him to stop by the market after work—
'Don't forget my meat,' she says, 'and get a jug of Coca Cola for Freddie.'
'Won't forget Ma,' Harry says, giving his wife a distant wink.
'I'm off to work now.'

Harry is now backing up his Plymouth sedan on the gravelly driveway.
As he passes the kitchen window, he honks to let Baba know he is almost gone.
Baba now opens the curtain in the breakfast room and waves to him.

Today Harry is especially proud of himself as he drives down Hoover Street.
He is beginning the week as a newly naturalized citizen of the United States.
Last Friday he was given his citizenship certificate in downtown Los Angeles.
For Harry, it was a day of mixed personal feelings in severing his British ties.
'I will always be an Englishman,' he said to Baba when she congratulated him.

Shiner and Geneva celebrated the occasion with cake, and a magic show.
Shiner told everyone he has taken up the hobby of 'prestidigitation.'
Freddie laughed and told him to do it in the big bathroom, 'whatever that is.'
Shiner then told Freddie he might disappear soon if he didn't shut up…

Harry was also recorded on the Philco record making machine—
Singing with his best Irish-English accent—the "Salvation Army Ballad."
Harry remembers it was a fun party on Friday night…

He now comes to a stop at Broadway and looks into his mirror.
He notices his former jet-black hair is changing to a light-gray color…

THE PINK OLEANDERS

He thinks he's worked too hard to pass his citizenship examinations…

Now he is driving south on Norwalk Boulevard towards Santa Fe Springs…
He recalls the tough times on the road after leaving Sydney Mines—
The vicissitudes he endured in search of a place to put down roots—

Now he admits to himself it was worth it— even the failures and the setbacks—
From Aspull to Wigan; then on to Sydney Mines, Nova Scotia —
Finally settling in Southern California in a place called Uptown—
It was indeed a dream journey for Harry, and now he was an American at last.
But inside his mind he cannot let go of one inescapable fact—
That he is now an upper, middle-class success story—
Living in a country he personally detests.

PHOEBE MOORE WITH HER HUSBAND, HARRY— CIRCA 1940

SCENE 24
"HOUND DOG" - SEPTEMBER 9, 1956

Baba has invited Fred, Pauline and the boys over tonight to see Elvis.
He will be on Baba's favorite TV program— the Ed Sullivan Show.

All have eaten take-out food in the breakfast room—
Breaded halibut—from Robinson's Restaurant, Pauline's favorite place for fish.
The youngest boy did not like his halibut, but he did like the french fries.

As all were finishing, Baba removed her false teeth and put them on the table.
The little boy saw this and screamed, while ducking under the table.
Baba laughed loudly and told Mikey to 'come up from there'—
'It's me dentures, Mikey!'
When he finally did raise his head, the boy refused to look at her and her teeth.
Instead, he stared at a clay rooster hanging on the breakfast room wall.
The rooster did not scare him as much as his toothless grandmother did...

Presently, Fred, Pauline and Paul are seated on Baba's front room couch...
The four-year-old boy is nervously lying on the green carpet in front of the TV.
He is still traumatized by the sight of Baba taking out her false teeth.
Shiner and Geneva are sitting in chairs brought in from the dining room.
Baba, as usual, is comfortably ensconced in her gray rocking chair...
Now Elvis appears in stark black and white on the big Philco TV screen...
He begins his performance with 'Don't be Cruel.'
The teenage girls in the audience scream like there's a fire in the theater.
Geneva says the screaming reminds her of the bobbysoxers and Frank Sinatra.
'Except Sinatra had talent,' Shiner says to his wife. 'Much more than this guy.'
Baba says she can't stand all the screaming... 'turn it off please...'
Shiner tells Baba it will all be over soon, and to relax. 'It's just music.'

Now Elvis is singing 'Hound Dog,' as the girls scream louder than ever…
Geneva says she likes 'Hound Dog' better than 'Mister Sandman.'
'Hey Mikey, what do you think of Elvis?' she asks, winking at the small boy.
The boy says Elvis is a good singer—'he makes the girls scream.'
Fred and Pauline laugh at the boy's response…

'I've had it,' says Baba, as she now gets up from her rocking chair.
'I can't stand it no more.'
She says good night to Elvis, and goes to her bedroom.
'There I will find some peace.'
Fred says Elvis will be a flash in the pan— 'here today, gone tomorrow…'
Pauline says Perry Como is a thousand times better than Elvis—
'I just don't get it,' she says. 'What do all those girls see in him?
He's icky looking.'

SCENE 25
"A REAL HULA SWEETHEART" - OCTOBER 25, 1940

Freddie is presently sitting inside Mount Olive Cemetery by himself.
The sun is setting in the west behind the profusion of walnut trees.
He has found Annie Simpson Scott's tombstone, and is resting by it.
He is thinking deeply about the changing world and the new military draft.
Part of him regrets studying for his naturalization papers.
But then again, part of him is thirsting for something beyond Uptown—
And now comes the time in his young life when the military life beckons.

Freddie now hears an owl above him hooting inside a walnut tree.
He senses a big change coming in his life, and he is okay with that.
He talked it over yesterday with his dad—
When the time comes, it will be the Army.
'At least I'll be standing on hard ground when I'm fighting,' he told his Ma.
Upon hearing Freddie's decision, Baba went into the water closet and cried.
Harry told his son he was proud of him for going in—
But that he disagreed with the draft.
'Imagine having a military draft in Sydney Mines,' he said to Purvis Spanks.'
Harry says fascism is 'a disease, just like the draft is a disease— 'No difference.'

Freddie is walking back home now from the cemetery.
As he turns right on Hoover, he notices all the pink oleanders in bloom—
Standing like giant pink bridesmaids in a gauzy dream wedding.
As he nears the front screen door, he can hear Hawaiian music playing.
Shiner is playing his 78 rpm record of "Iniki Malie" by Sol Hoopii.
Freddie comes inside now and starts to hula with an imaginary partner—
Now Shiner joins him, waving his hands like an Hawaiian dancer…
Geneva and Baba are laughing now as they emerge from the kitchen clapping.
Baba thinks the tall one is a 'real hula sweetheart.'

SCENE 26
"THE ELECTRIC MOMENT" - FEBRUARY 9, 1964

My brother has one of his car-club friends here tonight.
He is a bully hard-guy who likes to work on hot rods and cruise Greenleaf Ave.
As a member of my brother's car club, The Aztecs, he is the Master of Arms.
No one in their right mind would dare pick a fight with Big Dave Gregg…
I don't like Big Dave Gregg…

Tonight the Beatles are starring on the Ed Sullivan Show, and I will not miss it.
Now Big Dave says, 'I don't want to hear your screaming, Mikey.'
I plan to be excited seeing The Beatles, but I will keep my mouth shut…

Sitting on the front room sofa are my mother and father, and as usual,
They are smoking cigarettes and drinking cokes.
I am sitting on the green carpet, much like I did when Elvis came on in '56.
Except this time, the TV is beaming its cathode light from Baba's Wall…
I wonder what Baba would say about the Beatles if she were here still.
My mother thinks the Beatles are funny looking—
'Not sure about their music,' she says. 'But they sure need haircuts.'
Presently there is an advertisement playing on Channel 2…

Now the electric moment has arrived for seventy million people…
Ed Sullivan cannot contain the screaming. 'The Beatles!' he bellows…
The screaming inside the theater is deafening beyond compare…
Now they are playing "I Want To Hold Your Hand."
It seems all human time has stopped…
Now Big Dave says, 'What's with the mop tops? That's not rock music.
Paul says he prefers Peter, Paul and Mary, but admits 'these guys are okay.'
My cigarette-smoking mother thinks they're all 'icky-looking.'
I think this is the best rock band I've ever heard.

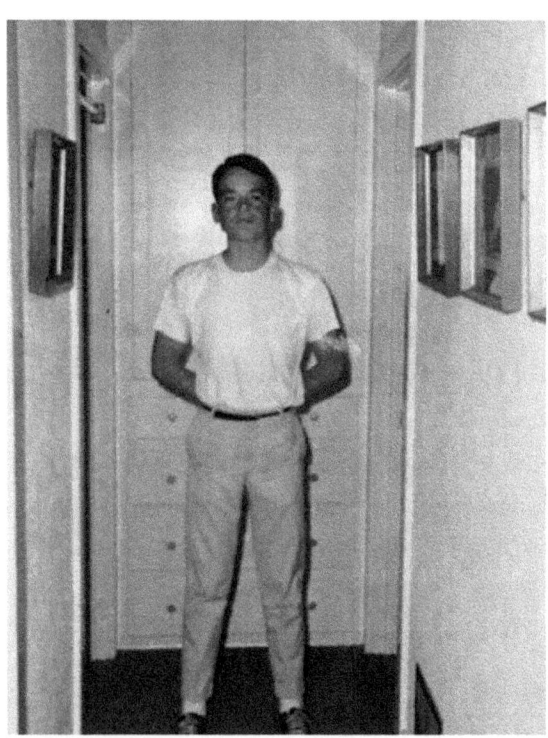

ONE OF TWO PHOTOGRAPHS IN EXISTENCE TAKEN INSIDE THE INNER HALLWAY OF THE HOOVER STREET HOUSE. THIS IS THE AUTHOR IN 1967. THE BIG BATHROOM IS AT LEFT, AND THE DOOR TO THE BASEMENT IS AT RIGHT, UNSEEN.

SCENE 27
"FREDDIE'S NEW GIRLFRIEND" - FEBRUARY 9, 1941

Harry is exhausted as he naps on Baba's new love seat in the front room.
She has decided to place this new furniture by the front door.

Florence, for one, thinks it's a bad place for a love seat—
'It's too breezy here,' she told Baba…
'Who can make love here by the damned front door?'
Baba said to 'hush Flo. I haven't any other place to put it for now…'

As Harry snores with noticeable congestion in his wheezing lungs,
Freddie and his new girlfriend, Pauline Williams, walk through the front door.
She is a tall brunette wearing a blue dress, revealing a 20 year-old girl's figure.
When she speaks, there is a noticeable mid-western twang to her voice.
Freddie is dressed in his usual church-going clothing— a white coat and a tie—
He is proud now to show off his beautiful girlfriend on this Sunday.

Harry is stirring now as Freddie brings Pauline into the dining room.
Baba walks out of the kitchen and shows genuine pleasure in greeting Pauline.
'Nice to meet you,' she says. 'Freddie has spoken of you many times!'
Harry walks in now, 'Looks like a movie star is here with us today, Ma.'
Pauline walks up to Harry now and hugs him with friendly affection.
'It's nice to meet you, sir,' she says, 'and happy Valentines to ya'll…'
Baba looks at Pauline, from head to toe, and now walks into the kitchen…
Geneva comes to Pauline now and shakes her hand. 'I'm Gene. Welcome.'

Baba is presently in the closed service porch, looking for a can of beans.
Harry comes in now and tells Baba he thinks Freddie has found 'thee one…'
Baba agrees, though she confesses she was hoping for an English girl…
'That girl, way she talks, sounds like she rolled into town with the Joads…'

THE PINK OLEANDERS

Harry laughs at the remark and tells Baba to not talk so loud…
'She may hear you…'

Freddie and Pauline are now embracing in Harry's den…
Freddie tells Pauline he thinks she's the prettiest girl he's ever seen…
Now he takes her behind the den door and kisses her.

Baba is calling for everyone to come to dinner…
'Freddie!…Pauline!…'Time to eat now!'
She will soon be serving Mackenflap in the dining room…

Pauline wants to know when he has to report for training.
Freddie says he has to report March 4th.
'I have to go to Nelles School to catch a bus there, then on to Camp Roberts.'
Pauline says she'll miss him when he goes away.

SCENE 28
"VIETNAM IS A TERRIBLE PLACE" - MAY 9, 1967

My mother is sitting in her big red chair in the front room…
She is reading the evening edition of The Uptown Daily News.
The bay window is fully open, as cars outside pass by on Hoover Street.
The afternoon sun is setting— casting a growing shadow on the lawn.

The TV is humming by Baba's Wall, where she liked to sit and rock.
My mom has the channel set to 4 for the NBC News.
She wonders how many kids will die in Vietnam this week?
'That man ought to be impeached for keeping this awful war going,' she says.
'I just hope,' she continues bitterly, 'that when that man is old and retired…
And he's sitting by the Pedernales, he'll think about all the kids he killed.'

My father is sitting in his big yellow chair across from my mother's.
He says getting angry and upset about it will do no good.
My mother says he's wrong—that people need to do something.
'What about your own sons, Fred,' she asks…
'Do you want them to go fight in Vietnam?'
My father says joining the army would do both boys a world of good—
'But you're right, honey' he injects. 'Vietnam is a terrible place.'

Now she notices an article in the newspaper about an old friend of Paul's—
Big Dave Gregg— who has been awarded the Purple Heart in Vietnam.
My father wonders what happened to him?
Now my mother says 'he was injured when a grenade exploded next to him…'
'It says a fellow Marine smothered the grenade with his body, and took the hit.'
My father is speechless…

SCENE 29
"HAWAIIAN MUSIC ON THE 4TH" - JULY 4, 1936

It seems Hoover Street is on fire with pink oleanders…
Every oleander tree on the street is in full summer bloom.
Presently, an artist has set up his easel at the corner by Broadway.
He is wearing a french beret, and enjoys talking to the curious.
Earlier Harry had visited the 'chap' and complimented his artwork…

If you look up Hoover Street, you can see many cars driving past on Beverly.
Those cars are heading to Uptown for the July 4th parade on Greenleaf.

Harry and Baba are celebrating the Fourth of July today with boiled lobsters.
Dinty and Kay are here with daughter Marilyn.
Baba is inside the front room making a fuss over her 'adorable' granddaughter…
Baba can't believe how big Marilyn is getting.
Shiner and Geneva, as usual, are outside, suntanning on top of the garage.
Shiner is serenading her with his Hawaiian steel guitar—
"My Little Grass Shack In Kealakekua Hawaii."

'I want to go back to my little grass shack in Kealakekua, Hawaii
I want to be with all the kanes and wahines that I knew long ago
I can hear old guitars a playing, on the beach at Hoonaunau…'
I can hear the Hawaiians saying "Komomai no kaua ika hale welakahao"
It won't be long 'til my ship will be sailing back to Kona…

Now Harry says he likes Geneva's new two piece swim suit.
Geneva smiles and says she bought it at Bullock's, just for him.
Shiner now reaches over and kisses Geneva, saying, 'Of course you did.'
Freddie is presently shooting baskets with his friend, David…
David tells Freddie he has a new girlfriend from church, named Eloise.

Freddie thinks David is now completely under his girlfriend's spell—
'Won't be long before she'll have you driving her to church every Sunday.'
'Well, that beats hanging out in the graveyard all the time,' says David…

Harry is now trimming the bougainvillea at the end of the driveway—
Like the blazing oleanders out front, this prized bush is in full bloom…
Harry planted it back in '31 to provide cool shade in the summer.
Now it is spreading on the roof like 'running blood on the battlements'—
As he works, Harry is singing the "Salvation Army Ballad."
Baba is coming out now, looking for Shiner…
'The lobsters is ready, boy.'
Shiner gets up from his lounge chair and scurries down the side ladder…
'Coming, Ma,' he says.

Now Baba is watering her prized rose bushes— seven 'Belles Portugaise—'
She is happy with their deep yellow blooms this spring…
Harry is coming over now with his trimming shears—
'Go lightly on the watering,' he says to Baba…
He tells her the fragrance of her 'Belles' is a sign of the presence of an angel…
'Straight from heaven above,' he tells her, as he kisses Baba on the cheek.
Baba says she loves 'the old cuckoo,' and that it is time to come in for dinner.

PHOEBE BLINKHORN OF INCE—CIRCA 1900

SCENE 30
"CARESSING IT LIKE A FOOTBALL" - JANUARY 25, 1969

Presently Teresa and I are necking inside the closed service porch…
She is wearing her tight-fitting, day-glo colored dress that makes her look sexy.
Two times now, Teresa has applied her special lipstick before kissing me again.
Her Slicker-mixed saliva tastes like cotton candy as we exchange tongues.
Embracing here unseen, we are like two birds under a midnight moon…

Now I have my hand on her firm butt, caressing it like a football…
Teresa loves the touch of my hand and kisses me with even more passion…
She is breathing heavy now, and is making her special love-making sounds—
An odd mix between painful groaning and pleasured giggling…

My desire now is to feel her breasts as we embrace here…
Slowly I lift my left hand, moving it torturously slow toward her right breast…
Now Teresa says we ought to go inside the water closet, 'for a little privacy…'
'Are we going to second base now?' I ask, as we shuffle inside, still kissing.
No answer this time…
'But…in here?'
The door closes…

VIEWING THE SERVICE PORCH FROM THE KITCHEN, 1967.

SCENE 31
"THE SHAKES" - MAY 1, 1941

Harry is presently sitting inside the water closet this evening.
He has a fever of 103 and is exhausted from working in the rain.
He wishes he still had his old job before the transfer to Ventura.
Baba made chicken soup for him but he couldn't stomach it.
He has been having the 'shakes' with extreme congestion in his lungs.
Lately he has been noticing blood in the toilet after peeing…

His thoughts are on God, and on his life, as he sits and shivers.
He realizes his health is not good presently.
Earlier, Baba asked him if he needed to go to Murphy Hospital for a check-up.
Harry told her no— that he was seen by a doctor up north—
'He said I was run down and in need of bedrest.'

Now Harry remembers the old glory days in Wigan and Sydney Mines…
Days when he would work ten hour days in the coal mines as a youth—
The time he was firing in Sydney Mines and saved the chap asleep on the tracks.
But most of all, he remembers his marriage in 1905 to Phoebe Blinkhorn…

'I'm so sick,' he says to himself.

BABA PICTURED IN THE BREAKFAST ROOM—1940'S

SCENE 32
"THE KISS INSIDE THE CLOSET" - FEBRUARY 19, 1943

Baba is presently setting the dining room table wth sandwiches and champagne.
Today is a rare, happy day for Baba—
Freddie and Pauline are getting married at St. Mary's this morning…

Flo and Irene are sitting in the front room listening to Viola play piano.
George is standing by the bay window, smoking a Chesterfield….
He exhales a large cloud of white smoke through the open side window.
Mister Cox is there, talking to his wife on their driveway.
George sees them and says, 'Sorry for all the pollution out there.'
Missus Cox comes to the window screen now and says, 'It's perfectly alright.'
'Oh George,' Mister Cox adds, 'How are things with the Fire Department?'
'Doing fine, sir,' George replies, 'I reckon smoke follows me wherever I go…'

Freddie is presently locked inside the big bathroom—
He is staring at himself in the mirror behind the sink…
Now he is talking to himself very quietly, so quietly, he can barely hear himself.
'I truly love Pauline with all my heart and soul— I think…'
Baba is knocking on the door, reminding Freddie he doesn't have much time.
'You need to be at the church in fifteen minutes, son,' she says. 'Hurry now.'
Geneva walks into Freddie's bedroom as he fixes his tie inside the closet…
Geneva finds him and offers to help him.
She is wearing a knee-length rayon dress with dark stockings and black shoes.
Freddie says she looks good as usual, and asks for the time.
Geneva winks and says he has ten minutes to get to the church.
Now she approaches Freddie and kisses him, saying… 'Congratulations.'
Her kiss was not intended to be so long and mushy…
But she enjoyed kissing Freddie again, and she knew he liked it again as well…

It is evening now, and Geneva and Shiner are having tea in the breakfast room.
Geneva thinks marriage will 'make our Freddie into a strapping man.'
Shiner laughs at Geneva and says, 'Strapping man, my foot…'
'The wind will surely blow Freddie clear across the sea.'
Geneva says it may be cold in Santa Barbara and hopes Pauline has a coat.
Shiner says he doubts they will be spending much time outdoors tonight…

Baba is presently inside the big bathroom, staring out the window…
She has moved the curtain a little so as to provide a clear view of the backyard.
Baba wonders who's on top of the garage at this hour?
She sees a man and a woman, and they are dancing close in the darkness.
Baba remembers when she was young, and 'spending time with wiry men.'
Now the dancing couple has disappeared from Baba's sight…

GENEVA AND BABA SUNTAN IN THE BACKYARD
SOMETIME IN THE 1940'S.

SCENE 33
"KEEP IT QUIET, FREDDIE" - JUNE 8, 1963

Geneva and Baba are in the front room yelling at each other…
Baba is saying that while in the process of moving out of the house last week, Geneva stole many of her good towels and bed sheets.

Geneva is denying it, saying, 'Phoebe, how can you say I stole from you?'
Now Baba is saying, 'My things is missing, and you took 'em!'
'Why on earth would I want your towels and your old bed sheets?'
Baba says Geneva has been stealing from her for years, 'ever since dad died.'

Shiner and Freddie are coming into the front room now from outside.
Shiner says he can hear them arguing in the backyard.
'What's the problem?'
Now both ladies are talking at the same time with loud anger…
Baba says she's had enough, and now wants to be wheeled into her bedroom.
Pauline now takes a crying Baba down the hallway to her room.

Freddie thinks it might have been someone else who did it—like Nurse Kathy.
Shiner nudges Freddie now and says it wasn't Nurse Kathy—
It was he who had taken the towels and the sheets—
'Keep it quiet, Freddie.'

Pauline now tells Freddie that it's between Phoebe and Geneva.
'Those two need to stop arguing,' she says. 'Phoebe may have a stroke over this.'
Freddie whispers into Pauline's ear…

SCENE 34
"MY GRANDCHILD MUST HAVE A FATHER" - SEPTEMBER 7, 1931

Baba is talking to daughter Florence in the breakfast room.
Flo has informed her mother she plans to elope with George in the morning.
There is silence for a full minute as Baba sips her tea…
And now Flo has something else to tell Baba…
'Me heart can't take it,' she says, 'What else now for Pete's sake?'
Flo looks her mother in the eye and says she's pregnant with George's child.

Baba now yells for Harry who is reading and smoking in the back den…
Harry is a bit startled to hear the loudness in his wife's voice.
He rises from his easy chair and travels through the house very concerned.
'What's going on here, Phoebe?' he says.
'Flo is eloping tomorrow, and she is expecting our first grandchild!'
Again, there is a silence in the breakfast room as Harry can't speak a word…

It is late evening now as Harry sits alone in the back den.
He is smoking his pipe and drinking his home brew with the back door open.
The cool night air is coming in through the screen door like a silent lover…
Harry wishes he and his family were still in Sydney Mines like old times.
Life was hard but much simpler than these strange times in the United States.

Now Harry shakes his head and continues to smoke his brown pipe.
As midnight strikes, he realizes it is time to let go of his only daughter—
Time for Florence to grow up and start a family, despite the coming hardships.
'This is indeed a blessing,' he decides. 'My grandchild must have a father.'
Baba comes into the den now and asks Harry when he's coming to bed.
Harry says having a daughter is as tough as mining coal on your back.
'It feels as though I've had the wind knocked out of me today,' he says.
Now Harry rises from his chair and hugs Baba with his long wiry arms.

THE FRONT SITTING ROOM—TAKEN IN 1968.
THE FIREPLACE WAS THE SETTING FOR TWO WEDDINGS— IN 1932 AND 1937.

SCENE 35
"THE TWENTY-THIRD PSALM" - MAY 2, 1941

Baba is sipping tea in the breakfast room on this overcast morning…
She is worried about Harry's persistent high temperature of 103.
Presently Harry is in the water closet sitting on the toilet.
He is feeling worse today than he did yesterday.
Once again he is peeing blood, and decides he needs to see the doctor soon.
Now he is muttering something from behind the locked door…
He is reciting from the Book of Common Prayer—
The Twenty-Third Psalm—

After flushing, Harry weakly opens the closet door and stands for a moment.
He wonders if he should say something to Phoebe, but decides not to.
Now he leaves the service porch, and heads for the bedroom to lie down.
It is 9:05 AM…

Harry is sweating as he lies on his back, staring up at the ceiling…
He wishes he hadn't worked overtime in the rain last week.
Now he closes his burning eyes and imagines being a young man again…
Back in the happy times with his young family in Sydney Mines…
Back to when Phoebe presented him with his first son in 1906…
He recalls the snow outside was piled three feet off the ground…
It was so cold inside their house, the midwife later caught pneumonia…
'Phoebe was so proud of that baby,' he remembers. 'Such a proud time.'
It is now 9:15 AM…

Harry now begins to weep in the awful stillness of the bedroom.
Inside his fevered mind, he sees strange sights and visions…
He sees his father, Connie, walking towards him in the Aspull snow…
'Hello son,' Connie says from 1887, 'Shall we go to Borsdane today?'

'I have a sack of dried pork bits for you, and this apple from Haigh.'
Harry extends his reaching arm for the imagined apple…
'Dad,' Harry says weakly, 'I don't want to die like this… not on my back…'
It is now 9:18 AM…

Harry now rises from his bed and steps slowly to the hallway…
He walks to the big bathroom and closes the door behind him.
As he steps before the sink and stares into the mirror,
He sees the face of a very sick Englishman from Lancashire…
He sees the eyes of a man in love with his pipe and his beer…
Presently, Francis Henry Moore collapses to the black-tiled floor…
It is now 9:20 AM…

THE SINK IN THE BIG BATHROOM WHERE HARRY DIED.
THIS WAS TAKEN IN 1967.

SCENE 36
"A FACE IN THE BEDROOM WINDOW" - JUNE 15, 1963

Here I am on top of this old garage...
I am sitting on the top rung of this side ladder.
I am scanning the dichondra lawn below, and the back windows of the house...
I can see a few oranges growing on the tree by the den window.
I can hear the repeating coos of the doves that sit on the power lines...
Beyond the house I see a grove of avocados, and beyond that—
Mount Olive Cemetery...
From up here, that graveyard looks dark and creepy.
No one gets buried in there anymore...

Now the radio is playing inside the back den— my room...
I climbed down to turn it on because I was bored just sitting up here.
The dial on my clock radio is set to KRLA as always...
But I can barely hear it from up here.
I need to turn it up higher...

There, that's better. it's on full blast now...
The Essex is singing "Easier Said Than Done."
That's the best song on the radio right now...

Now there is a face in Baba's bedroom window looking out...
I can see two eyes and a nose, staring from behind the transparent curtain.
Those two black eyes and the unsmiling face belong to Baba...
I think my loud radio is bothering her...
Now Lonnie Mack is on, playing "Memphis."
Baba is still looking at me from behind the window curtain...
I think she is crying.

SCENE 37
"KISSING IN THE WATER CLOSET" - JANUARY 25, 1969

Teresa and I are kissing like crazy inside this old water closet…
It was her big idea to come inside here to make out in private.
I have managed to unzip her dress down to her waist.
I can see her white bra strap encircling her brown back.
It is definitely a big turn-on…
Teresa is now unbuttoning my shirt and kissing my neck.
I love it when she licks and sucks the skin around my ears…

Now we are exchanging wet tongues french-style, with eyes closed…
She's pushing her hardened breasts up against my chest.
I enjoy hearing Teresa moan like a sex-crazed Ann Margaret…
I must be in a James Bond movie…

Teresa is presently mindless, as she kisses my mouth like a repeating robot…
Now all the sudden she stops her wild necking frenzy…
She sees something interesting lying on top of the toilet tank—
An old copy of the English Book of Common Prayer…
'A prayer book,' she says. 'in here?'

'How old is this book?' she asks, as she picks it up.
'I don't know.' I answer. 'It's been in here for as long as I can remember.'
'It says 1928 on the copyright page,' Teresa whispers…

Now I am losing patience…
I get behind her and start to lift her dress above her waist.
As her skirt rises to reveal a pair of bikini panties underneath—
She suddenly stops me…
'No, no Mikey,' she says, as she grabs my hands.

'I don't think I'm ready for this… not yet.'
'This is all too fast and too scary,' she says, as she lowers her skirt back down.
'God will decide, my love, if we should ever go to second base.'
'Would you like to pray now, Mikey?'
I said sure, and she prayed to Jesus for spiritual guidance.
I prayed to Jesus privately, asking for Teresa to soon put out.

SCENE 38
"THESE CHERRIES IS RIPE" - OCTOBER 13, 1946

Freddie and Pauline are suntanning on top of the garage this afternoon...
Both went to Mass earlier with Shiner, Geneva and Baba.
Shiner drove them all in his Model A, honking his horn three times at people—
Just to annoy Baba...
After Mass they all went to Jack's for breakfast...

Pauline is dressed in her one-piece bathing suit, revealing a noticeable cleavage.
Freddie is wearing the white trunks he bought last summer in Santa Barbara...
Both look bronzed and shapely as they lie on aluminum lounges facing west...
Freddie is poking his index finger into Pauline's side, making her giggle.
Her breasts shake like two big melons in a bag, so Freddie keeps poking her...

Freddie says he dreamed of this day many times during the war years—
Dreamed of being with his girl, and relaxing under the Southern California sun.
He says when he was on his way to Kiska, he shook from fear for four days.
Pauline says she can imagine how scary it must have been waiting to land...
'Thank God,' she exclaims. 'the Japs left right before you arrived!'
Freddie says he was lucky, but even luckier to have her as his wife.
Pauline says she loves him more than 'all the stars in the sky, forever and a day.'
Now Freddie pokes Pauline again and again...

Shiner and Geneva are coming down the driveway now...
They too are wearing bathing suits, with Geneva dressed in her new bikini.
Harry allows Geneva to go up the side ladder first...
He watches directly from below as Geneva slowly climbs each rung—
One toenail-polished foot at a time...
Harry says, 'These cherries' is ripe for the picking today...'
Geneva says, 'Shiner, watch what you say. Freddie and Pauline are up here.'

THE PINK OLEANDERS

Baba is presently in the big bathroom.
She faces the mirror, studying her skin and eyes.
She is alarmed at the size of the goiter in her neck today.
'Too much bacon in the Potato Dish last night,' she says to herself…
Now she turns to the window, and partly opens the curtain.
She sees her two boys on the garage rooftop enjoying their sexy wives…
'Youth is such a strong drink,' she says to herself.
'I miss my Harry today…'

Freddie and Pauline are presently down in the basement…
They have decided to share drinks and cigarettes in private.
Shiner and Geneva have taken Baba out for a drive in the Model A.
Freddie is pouring wine from one of the dozen bottles stored down here.
Pauline is standing with her legs crossed as she smokes a Chesterfield.
She is wearing a short black skirt and a white low-cut blouse.
In her hair is a white ribbon, knowingly put there to be untied…

The Philco Hi-Fi is playing upstairs in the dining room.
Freddie has the radio dial set to station KFI.
Pauline says she likes Glenn Miller music. It makes her happy.
Freddie pours her another glass of wine, saying she makes him happy…
'My dad drank so much beer down here,' Freddie says.
'He was the King of Kegs!'
Now as he grows more tipsy, Freddie can't keep his eyes off his wife's big breasts.
Pauline is enjoying her drink and the way her husband is looking at her…
She knows what Freddie wants tonight, and now, as Artie Shaw wails upstairs,
Pauline drunkenly turns around and faces the wall…

PAULINE AND FREDDIE, WITH GENEVA, STANDING ON THE COX FRONT PORCH—EARLY 1940'S.

SCENE 39
"FLIRTING IN THE GRAVEYARD" - MARCH 30, 1935

It is sunset and Freddie is running through the dark graveyard at Mount Olive.
Shiner's new girlfriend, Geneva, is searching for him in a game of Hide 'N Seek.
Shiner is working at the bank today until 6 o'clock.
Geneva got off an hour early at the fruit packing company on Magnolia Street.
Now Freddie is hiding behind the David Morris tombstone…

Here comes Geneva wearing shorts, a white cotton blouse with a pink scarf.
Her bare legs are tanned and muscular as she comes near…
Freddie jumps out now and screams in hopes of frightening her.
Geneva laughs instead, and allows Freddie to take her into his arms…
The 17 year old high school senior now kisses the 20 year old Nebraska girl…
Only the dead around them— and the walnut trees—
Can claim to have seen this lost kiss…

Geneva is shocked Freddie kissed her—
But thinks he kisses well for a high school boy.
Freddie wants to continue the 'secret kissing game in the old graveyard.'
'Tell me,' he says with open arms, 'which of these departed will tell on us?'
Geneva smiles now, takes her pink scarf off, and lets it fall to the ground…
It is night time presently, and Harry is saying grace at the dining room table…
Shiner, Freddie, Flo and little Irene are all seated around it.
'Bless this house, and the good people in it,' Harry prays.
'And bless King George too…'

Geneva is in the kitchen heating up dinner rolls in Baba's white oven…
Flo says she wishes Irene's weight would increase a little…
'She's as skinny as a termite—eats like one—that's for sure.'
Harry jokingly says to give her some of his beer—

'That'll put some poundage on her.'

Baba is now serving baked ham with apple sauce and green beans…
She tells Harry to light the candles on the table.
Using a Bailey's Liquor matchbook, he quickly lights the two red candles.
Geneva comes out of the kitchen now with her hair slightly disheveled…
Baba says Geneva needs a new hair stylist. 'Are them rolls done yet?'
Shiner laughs and says even with her hair a little mussed, she's still beautiful.
Freddie says he thinks Shiner is still beautiful too.
'Look at him, Ma, he's as pretty as his sister.'

Geneva says she thinks the rolls will be done in five minutes…but maybe not.
Now Baba barks out, 'How long does it take to bake 'em in Nebraska?'
Everyone around the table is laughing now as Geneva stands by Shiner…
'Oh, I don't know,' Geneva answers shyly. 'Mother always cooked for us girls.'
Now Baba notices a red mark on Freddie's neck…
'Boy, what's that bruise there on your neck,' Baba asks.
'Looks like it hurts.'
'It's nothing Ma,' Freddie answers.
'I got it horsing around in the graveyard with David.'
Now Harry asks for someone to please pass him the ham, 'and the beans too.'

FREDDIE AND DAVID HORSING AROUND AT SUNSET
AT MOUNT OLIVE CEMETERY IN 1935

SCENE 40
"THAT POOR MAN" - NOVEMBER 22, 1963

When school let out at three o'clock today, I walked home in a daze…
Kennedy was killed this morning, and I felt mostly sad and scared.
When I walked by the old graveyard on Broadway, I stopped and looked in.
As always, the grounds were littered with trash and dead weeds.
Sometimes when I stand at the gate, I can hear voices whispering to me…

Now my parents and I are in the front room, watching the TV.
My mother has it set to Channel 4, with Huntley and Brinkley reporting.
My father is still dressed in his suit, while my mother is wearing a blue dress.
They are both smoking cigarettes and drinking bottled Cokes—
Both are staring shocked at the television screen by the front door…
"This is just awful,' my mother says, wiping her eyes with a kleenex—
'That poor man…'
'This is one of the worst tragedies in American history.'

Now my father wants to know what we're having for dinner tonight.
My mom says she doesn't know.
Because of the news today, she hasn't thought about it.
'How 'bout Tastee Freez?'
'Good idea,' he says. 'What does everyone want?'
Paul walks in now from the hallway asking what's for dinner.
My father says we're having Tastee Freez tonight.
Paul says he wants 'a hot dog, chili fries and a cherry coke.'
My mother says she is craving a large cheeseburger with onions, and some fries.
I tell my father I want a hot dog with ice cream.
'Ice cream doesn't come with it, Mick,' he says. 'I'll get you fries.'
Now Paul says he wants a strawberry shake to go with his hot dog…
'I say, 'Me too, dad! I want a shake too. Chocolate.'

THE PINK OLEANDERS

Now Paul says he wants to change his order to fried shrimp.
I say, 'Me too, I want shrimp.'
My father gets up from the sofa now and says he'll go get dinner…
'Want to come, Mikey?'

SCENE 41
"THE BABY WEIGHED IN AT 18 POUNDS" - JULY 14, 1947

Baba is presently in the breakfast room talking on the phone.
Freddie is on the other end of the line calling from Murphy Hospital—
'It's a boy,' he says through the phone receiver.
Baba says, 'Oh Freddie, that's wonderful! Did you name him yet?'
Freddie says he thinks Pauline wants to name the boy, Paul.
Baba says, 'I like it, Freddie. Paul is a good biblical name.'

Now she asks if the 'new mother' is in good shape after her labors.
Freddie says he doesn't know because the baby weighed in at 18 pounds.
Baba tells Freddie to stop his kidding, and to tell her 'the Lord's truth'…
'Pauline is fine,' Freddie says laughing. 'The baby is 7 pounds 15 ounces…'
'We couldn't be happier, Ma!'…

Baba hangs up the phone and goes to the basement door.
Now she is descending the basement steps, passing dozens of canned goods…
She reaches the bottom and heads for a locked cabinet…
It is located directly beneath the wooden landing of the steps…
With a skeleton key, she unlocks the padlock and opens the creaking door…

This, Gentle Reader, is the darkest, creepiest place in the entire house—
This rank basement crawlspace— that has, perhaps, never seen the light of day.
There is no light switch inside— just the smell of old fermentations.

Now Baba pours from an old bottle of Harry's home-brew into a one-shot glass.
She raises it up— toasting the arrival of a new grandchild.
'To you, Paul,' she says aloud. 'I drink this in your name—'
'And in your grandfather's name too.'
She wishes Harry could be here to drink this toast with her today….

DINT, FREDDIE, BABA AND SHINER PICTURED IN THE BACKYARD, 1940.

SCENE 42
"THREE KNOCKS" - OCTOBER 31, 1933

It is a quarter to midnight, and Harry is reading in his den…
He has an old copy of the North Sydney Herald in hand.
There is a single light on, coming from the brightly lit candle on his desk.
Harry is drawing happily on his pipe, filled with his special smoking blend.
Now he checks the clock that is ticking on the wall…
Baba has been in bed since ten, and Missus Clancy turned in shortly after that.
Shiner and Freddie are still out, 'doing only the devil's business—them two!'

Now there are three knocks sounding on his outside door…
Harry takes in one more draw from his pipe and gets up…
He opens the door to find Katie Mae on the steps wearing her night clothes.
'Come in, Katie Mae,' Harry says, 'Come in out of the cold…'

Harry and Missus Clancy are now seated in his candle-lit den…
They are presently talking about her troubled marriage…
Katie Mae says she wishes she felt more comfortable being a wife.
'Jim is a wonderful husband…he truly is, but he's never home anymore…'
'He's been out of work for months, poor soul, but he keeps trying.'
Now Katie Mae starts to weep quietly in the darkness…
She tells Harry how lonely she has been since getting married to Jim at age 17.
'I need a man's touch, a man's embrace more, much more, than his baby.'
'All I do is work like someone's old dog, cleaning and cooking and washing.'
Harry now puts his sympathetic hand on Missus Clancy's shoulder….
'Please Mister Moore,' she says crying now. 'Please take me away from all this.'

Harry tells his midnight guest to calm herself, and to listen to him for a minute.
'When I left Sydney Mines in '21, I was out on the road for two years…'
'I experienced happy times, and also horrible times of which I cannot describe.'

'But what kept me going was my family— my wife and the four children.'
'I kept them inside my mind like a treasure—'
'Even as I rode the rails through Saskatchewan and Alberta…'
'Truly Katie Mae, without that one vital anchor in life— the family— well…'
'There is very little reason for moving forward in all things…'

Now Harry stands and brings Missus Clancy to her feet…he embraces her…
This touch of a man, now, as I touch you, is just a passing thing, Katie.
'Like the wind, it comes and goes, and no one knows how or where.'
'But back home is Jim, your life and your anchor…'
'He is waiting for you to return— to believe in him again…'
Missus Clancy now lifts her face to Harry—
She is looking to him for something he can't give.
Harry winks, and releases his embrace.

SCENE 43
"INSTEAD OF TWO GUYS WRESTLING, I SEE FOUR" - APRIL 13, 1951

Freddie, Pauline and Paul are visiting tonight to see Uncle Shiner's new TV set.
He bought it at Sears in downtown Los Angeles for two hundred dollars.
Now it is hooked up to the new antenna on the roof next to the chimney...

Uncle Shiner says we will all be watching live television for the first time.
He has the dial set to KTLA, Channel 5, for the Hollywood Wrestling Show...
Baba is excited as she sits in her rocking chair by the front door.
'Turn it on now, son,' she says impatiently.
Finally, the little screen illuminates, like one of Shiner's magic tricks...
Everyone in the front room is now oohing and aahing at the amazing sight...

Baba says she's never seen bigger boys in her whole life...
Geneva says the wrestlers have big muscles and tight-fitting trunks...
'I wonder what Father Heidker would say about these guys on television.'
'Is this a sin?' Geneva asks.
Baba tells Gene to not worry about it, to just watch the show, and be quiet...

Pauline is sitting on the sofa with little Paul and Freddie...
She says the black and white picture is not clear or focused.
'Is it broken,' she asks?
Shiner says the TV is new and that it is not broken...
'It could be the antenna on the roof,' he says. 'Maybe it's not connected right.'

Pauline is squinting her eyes now—
As she watches Lou Thesz manhandle his opponent...
Geneva says the picture is blurry...
She asks Shiner to go outside and jiggle the antenna wire.
Pauline says, 'That's a good idea, Shiner. Maybe doing that would fix the thing.'

Shiner now exits the front door with a flashlight and goes to the side window.
He finds the antenna wire and starts to shake it.
'Does that help?' he asks.
Baba says for Shiner to 'fix it quick, son. I can't see the television at all!'

Shiner has retrieved a ladder, and has now climbed up on the roof.
Freddie has also gone outside to steady Shiner's ladder…
Shiner now pulls the ladder up to the roof, and sets it against the chimney.
As Shiner climbs, shining his flashlight, he sees nothing but stars in the sky…
Freddie says for Shiner to 'be careful up there.'
Pauline comes to the side window and says the picture is awful…
'Instead of two guys wrestling, I see four…'

Geneva gets up and starts to turn the control knobs on the front of the set.
She turns the left knob to the right, and then the right knob to the left…
She doesn't touch the center knob, saying, 'I'm not sure what this knob does…'
'What are you doing, Gene?' Baba yells from her chair. 'You made it worse.'
Now the picture is rolling on the screen like an out-of-order slot machine…

It is half past nine o'clock.
The wrestling matches on Channel 5 have gone off the air…
Shiner says it took some doing to finally fix the TV picture, but he managed.
Geneva giggles and says she doesn't know how Shiner does it all the time…
'He can fix anything that breaks,' she says with pride.
Pauline says she could see the wrestlers much better after Shiner fixed it.
'It was like I was at the Olympic, watching these guys right next to me!'
Freddie now says, 'television is the greatest invention mankind has ever seen.'
Pauline says she wishes the Hollywood Wrestling show was still on…
'Those big boys sure know how to take care of themselves.'

SHINER WITH HIS HAWAIIAN GUITAR— TAKEN IN THE 1930'S

SCENE 44
"PROFESSOR QUIZ" - AUGUST 7, 1940

Harry is in the dining room smoking his pipe.
He is listening to the Professor Quiz radio program on the Philco.
Baba is in the kitchen making Mackenflap…

Now she is making a loud racket with the pots and pans in the service porch.
Harry says he has never heard such a loud noise in all his days.
Baba says he is exaggerating… 'I make noise all the time for Pete's sake…'

'A man walks one-fourth of a block—
Then retraces one-half of the distance—or sixty feet—
How many feet will he then walk to reach the end of the block?'

Harry draws in his special smoking blend and ponders the possible answer…
He knows the key to the right answer is using logic, and sound mathematics…

Harry thinks he may be thinking too hard and now calls on Baba…
'If any person can solve this, I pick Phoebe Blinkhorn from Ince.'

Harry repeats the question for Baba to ponder…
'Ahh, yes,' she says smiling, 'that's 420, dear. Dinner's done.'
Harry draws again from his pipe, jealous of his wife's 'mental gifts.'

Shiner and Geneva come in through the front door with two jars of Coca Cola.
Geneva asks Harry what's on the radio right now…
Harry says he is listening to the Professor Quiz program from New York…

'A woman is 86 years old; she is 3/4 as old as her husband—
If their child is one eighth as old as the father—

How old was the father when the child was born?'

Harry asks Geneva what she thinks the answer might be…
Geneva says, 'let me think, what is one eighth of 86 years?'
Shiner says Geneva is thinking about it, and that is a good thing…
Geneva says the answer is 22… 'that's when most men become fathers.'
Now Baba laughs loudly at Geneva's answer. 'It's 42, girl.'
'The husband is 48 years old,' she says.
'Just subtract 6…one eighth of 48…and you get 42.'
Harry draws again from his smoking pipe.
He's quite impressed with his wife's 'mental faculties.'

SCENE 45
"HER GROOVY DAY-GLO" - FEBRUARY 14, 1969

It is Valentines Day, and it is Friday night…
Teresa is looking groovy tonight…looking far out—
Wearing her pink Day-Glo dress…
I like this dress the best because it fits tightly around her butt.

Presently she is inside my bedroom closet.
She's looking into a mirror as she applies Slicker lipstick.
When she does that, that is her signal to me—
That it is time to do some serious french-kissing.
She says she wants me to come inside now…
Before I do, I want to put some music on as we make out in the closet…

Let's see…

The Mothers of Invention, Freak Out?
Naw… Too weird. Not good for kissing anybody…
The Beach Boys, Pet Sounds?
Naw…Not groovy at all…Surf music is not cool!
Bob Dylan, Blonde on Blonde?
Naw…His voice is grating, and Teresa doesn't dig him…
The Beatles' White Album?
Naw… I have played that album to death already…
The Doors is a very far out band, and so, yes, I will play their first album…
"The End" is the coolest song on this LP.
It is perfect for making out with your chick in the dark…

Now I am french-kissing Teresa inside my walk-in closet.
The door is closed…

The Doors are playing their guitar-droning masterpiece of insanity…
Robby Krieger is lacerating the walls of my bedroom with his electric guitar…

Surrounding our embracing bodies are my school clothes and shoes.
I haven't done my laundry yet this weekend so I can smell the sweat in them.
Teresa is too busy french-kissing me like a woodpecker to notice the odor.
Now I am licking her quivering neck as I slowly unzip her Day-Glo dress …
'Shug Shug,' she says, frenching me again, 'You turn me on so much!'

Ray Manzarek's slithering organ now shakes the room with a loud hum…
Teresa is allowing me to unzip her Day-Glo all the way down to her waist.
I can see her white panties underneath her darkened pantyhose…
She opens her mouth now, begging for my tongue to enter into hers…

Now I am lifting her Day-Glo above her waist—
She shudders as I caress her firm butt.
Her sheer pantyhose is electric to the touch…
I am presently getting a hard-on as we make out—here in this old closet…
Teresa has my tongue inside her wet swishing mouth, sucking on it gently…
I like the feel of her butt, and wish now to feel her breasts, if she'll let me…

I ask Teresa if maybe we can 'twine our way to second base tonight'—
After all, 'it is Valentine's Night, and as they say, love is in the air'…
'Shug, Shug,' she says, 'You turn me on so much I can't stand it.'
'I want to marry you someday,' she says as she kisses my neck.
'I want to marry you too, Goobe,' I say. 'But what about second base tonight?'

Now Teresa stops kissing me and looks into my mirror…
Again she is putting on more lipstick, which means she's not done tonight.
'I still think,' she says, 'that our relationship is perfect— at first base'…
'I understand,' I say, 'but can I at least see your bra? I promise not to touch!'

Now there is a loud knock on the bedroom door…
It is my mother demanding that I unlock my door. 'Is Teresa in there?'
Teresa and I quickly walk out of the closet…
It takes two attempts for me to zip up her groovy Day-Glo.

SCENE 46
"LET THEM DANCE, DEAR" - DECEMBER 8, 1941

Freddie is kissing Pauline inside his bedroom closet on this cold morning…
They plan to go to the movies at the Uptown Roxy Theater.
Because of the Japanese attack yesterday at Pearl Harbor in Hawaii,
Freddie has been ordered to report to the Nelles School at 4 this afternoon.
There he will board an Army bus headed to Fort Ord, California.
But for now he has the gorgeous Pauline Williams in his arms, kissing him.

Baba now comes into Freddie's bedroom, wondering where they are.
'Freddie, Pauline,' she calls out. 'Are you two in here?'
Freddie steps out of his closet and says Pauline is helping him with his hair.
Baba says to come quickly to the dining room…
'Shiner has the radio hooked up to Roosevelt's speech before Congress.'
'Come listen…'

'Yesterday, Dec. 7, 1941 - a date which will live in infamy - the United States of America was suddenly and deliberately attacked by naval and air forces of the Empire of Japan…'

As FDR speaks on the radio, everyone is seated around the table…
There's Shiner sitting next to Geneva, who is sitting next to Pauline…
Freddie is holding hands with Pauline, as Baba sits next to the Coxes—
And they are sitting next to the Philco Radio, listening with closed eyes…

Baba wonders what Dad Moore would say about yesterday's attack.
Mister Cox says Harry would be angry, and would support war against Japan.
'I wish he were here today,' she says, 'He'd tell us what this is all about…'

It is ten minutes later and the United States has now declared war against Japan.

THE PINK OLEANDERS

Shiner says since we are at war now, we might as well play some music…
Presently he is putting one of his 78 rpm records on the Philco turntable—
Artie Shaw playing 'Stardust" from the Blue Room in New York…

Now Shiner and Geneva are dancing on the green carpet in the front room…
They look great together as they join arms and move to the beat of the music…
Geneva giggles now as Shiner twirls like a ballerina for a few moments…
Freddie laughs and presently takes Pauline into his arms—
They too are swinging and swaying on the green carpet…
Baba is clapping her hands now as her boys dance with their sweethearts…
Mister and Missus Cox smile happily as they watch, but decline to join them…
'Maybe this is not a good time to dance,' he says to his wife.
'Many will die in this war.'
Missus Cox turns to her husband and says, 'Let them dance, dear.'—
'It will give them a reason to fight.'

FRED, MIKE, BABA AND PAUL, TAKEN IN 1953;
HARRY'S DEN IS SEEN IN THE BACKGROUND.

SCENE 47
"HARRY DOESN'T LOOK GOOD" - MAY 2, 1941

Come inside, my friend…
Go left under the arch and head for the green-carpeted hallway …
Something very wrong is going on inside there…
That's Baba wailing and screaming like she's been stabbed by someone…
No need to rush in there…
She needs to understand that her life has changed forever…
Her husband, Harry, is lifeless on the bathroom floor…
It is 9:25 in the morning on this overcast Friday…

Baba is now on the phone…
She is telling Uncle Willie that 'something's awfully wrong with Harry'—
That he passed out on the bathroom floor and isn't breathing…
'Please Willie,' she pleads. 'Come up here quick!'

Now Baba runs outside and goes next door to the Cox house.
She rings their doorbell three times before Mister Cox opens the door.
Baba is near fainting as she explains what is happening next door…
Mister Cox puts his coat on and follows Baba to the house.
When he gets to the big bathroom, he sees Harry lying on the black tile—
His face pointing up to the ceiling; his eyes still open…
Mister Cox places his fingers on Harry's neck to find a pulse, and finds none.
'We need to move him into the bedroom,' he says.
'Harry doesn't look good.'

Uncle Willie comes into the house now and heads for the big bathroom…
Baba is telling him Harry is dead—
She says he's been awfully sick and run-down from working in the rain…
'He's dead, Willie…My Harry, he's dead…'

Uncle Willie finds his brother on the bathroom floor and tries to rouse him.
Like Mister Cox, he places two fingers on Harry's neck, hoping for a pulse…
Now he and Mister Cox pick up Harry by his arms and legs.
They struggle in taking him down the hallway and into the big bedroom…
Baba is wailing loudly as she motions them to put Harry on the bed…
They carefully place Harry on his back…
Mister Cox tells Uncle Willie to close Harry's eyes… 'Let him rest.'
Now Baba sits by Harry on the side of the bed—
Her head resting on his chest….
Mister Cox and Uncle Willie quietly step out of the big bedroom…

It is evening time presently, and Father Heidker is visiting with Baba.
They are sitting on the love seat by the front door—
Baba is holding a tissue as Father Heidker reads from a pocket prayerbook…

'In your hands, O Lord,
We humbly entrust our brothers and sisters.
In this life you embraced them with your tender love;
Deliver them now from every evil
And bid them eternal rest…'

HARRY IN THE OIL FIELDS OF SANTA FE SPRINGS—CIRCA 1924

SCENE 48
"RITZ CRACKERS" - SEPTEMBER 25, 1963

Baba's funeral is finally over, and all the relatives are here for the reception…
There's Uncle Shiner with Aunt Geneva sitting by the fireplace.
He's showing Geneva a card trick that has completely fooled her…
'Oh Shiner,' she says in amazement. 'How did you do that?'

Uncle Dint and Aunt Kay are sitting by the bay window—
They are dressed in black, eating cold-cuts and Ritz crackers…
Their daughters Marilyn and Susie are seated as well—
They too are eating Ritz crackers…
Aunt Flo and Uncle George are sipping Sanka coffee in the breakfast room…

She tells George she's starving.
She wonders why Pauline doesn't have the main food out yet.
George says she's needs to be patient and to have some hors d'oeuvres for now.
'Cold-cuts and Ritz crackers?' she says, 'At my mother's funeral reception?'
'Not a chance!'

Uncle Willie and Aunt Annie are sitting at the dining room table.
They are eating salami cold-cuts with Ritz crackers and mozzarella cheese.
They are talking to Freddie and Pauline about the gravesite and the funeral.
Freddie says the cemetery grounds crew will maintain the gravesite at no cost.
Uncle Willie says the funeral service was done quite well by Father Elliot.
But says he disliked having Geneva wail so loudly at the casket like she did…
Pauline says she agrees…
'Gene went overboard with her fake crying thing.'

Aunt Flo has just walked in and is asking when dinner will be served.
Pauline looks surprised and says there will be no dinner served…

Just cold-cuts, cheese slices and crackers…
'All of this has been so sudden on us,' Pauline says, 'Eat all you want.'
Aunt Flo now says, 'Are you kidding? Ritz crackers at my mother's funeral?'
Pauline now stands up and puts her hands on her hips—
'Excuse me, Florence?'
Flo looks at Pauline, shakes her head, and walks back into the breakfast room…

I am the eleven year old boy sitting on top of the garage roof…
Coming up here is good for escaping the crowd inside the house.
I feel sad and sick as I sit up here on the top rung of this old ladder—
I'm looking at the orange trees, the grass, and Baba's roses.
Staring down from here, I can see Baba's "1953" carved in the cement walkway.
Sometimes I think about the old times when I was a little kid…
Those old times are like old records you play on a record player…
They make you feel homesick deep inside…

The sky is not blue today because of the brown smog.
A freight train is presently crossing Broadway Street below Magnolia Avenue…
As it barrels along on the steel rails, I can hear the grating of the train wheels…
Overhead I see another fast-moving jet, heading west to LA airport…

Now I can hear Paul playing a record inside his bedroom…
He is playing "Stranger On The Shore" by Acker Bilk…
Sometimes when I look to the bedroom window, I think I can see Baba there—
Her stern face staring outward from behind the lace curtain—
I can't believe she is gone.

AUNT FLO AND GEORGE; TAKEN IN THE 1940'S. MISTER COX'S HOUSE IS NEXT DOOR.

SCENE 49
"IN THE ART DECO DARKNESS" - APRIL 1, 1931

Today is move-in day for Harry and Phoebe Moore of Hillview Court.
For eight years Phoebe has scrimped on every dollar earned—
And saved up every dime…
Now after 13 months of construction on nearby Hoover Street,
The Moore's are finally moving into their big new house by the cemetery.
Freddie says he loves living next to the spookiest graveyard in America.

Florence thinks the new house is 'big, but it needs another bathroom.'
Harry reminds his daughter of the water closet inside the service porch area.
'Yes dad,' she says, 'But there's no bathtub in there…'

Dinty and Shiner are now lugging in Baba's new sofa into the front room.
'Put it against that wall,' Baba says, pointing to the west wall.
'That's where I'll sit every morning.'
Shiner says the sofa is too hard for anyone to sit on, much less lay on…
Baba says for Shiner to hush up—
'There better not be any laying going on in this house, tell you for sure.'
Shiner laughs and says she ought to 'tell that to Dinty and Kay, for sure, Ma.'
Freddie tells his Ma he likes her new sofa.
'It's perfect for trampolining, Ma.'
'Not on your life, son,' Baba says with a wink—
'Not if you want me to bake for you…'

Baba is now scrubbing the black and green-colored tiles in the big bathroom.
She has a can of Old Dutch Cleanser in hand as she cleans the walls.
Harry says he needs to borrow the Old Dutch so he can clean the toilet.
He now walks down the hallway to the door leading to the service porch.

He opens it and sees daughter Florence standing by the back door.
She's looking out the window and can see a funeral procession on Broadway.
'Gives me the creeps, dad,' she says, 'living by that graveyard over there.'
'This land was what your ma and I could afford, Flo,' he says.
'Land by a graveyard is cheaper.'
'Well, I'm moving out first chance I get, with George,' she says.
'We're getting married, dad… Not much you and ma can do about it'…

Harry enters into the new water closet and cleans the toilet.
He stands on the toilet seat and cleans the art deco light fixture above the door.
Harry reaches into his pocket for his copy of the Book of Common Prayer—
He wipes down the toilet tank with the rag, and places the book there.

Baba walks into the water closet now and closes the door behind her.
Harry is startled by her abrupt intrusion, and asks what she is doing.
Baba says for Harry to kiss her now— on this first day in the new house.
'For good luck, Harry.'
Harry turns around and smiles at his wife.
He turns off the light and kisses Baba in the art deco darkness…

PART TWO
"THE PINK OLEANDERS"

FREDDIE SHOOTING BASKETS IN THE BACKYARD — LATE 30'S

SCENE 50
"I'M BLIND, MA!" - JANUARY 11, 1952

Baba is wearing her black and white polkadot dress and black dress shoes.
She is going shopping for the day with Geneva and Aunt Annie.
They plan to go to Bullocks in Los Angeles, then on to Clifton's for lunch.

As Baba secures her stockings to her garter belt, she hears the phone ringing.
She moves quickly down the hallway to the breakfast room to answer it...
She is mindful that Freddie took Pauline to the Hospital last night in labor...

Now it is Fred with the news that it is a boy again; eight pounds and six ounces.
'He was born at eight twenty this morning...just an hour ago,'
'Oh Freddie, son,' Baba says happily. 'What will you name this boy?'
'I like the name, Mike,' Freddie says.
'I like that name, Fred,' Baba says. 'When can I see him?'
Freddie tells his mother they will be over on Sunday with the new baby...
'Alright Freddie,' Baba says, 'We'll see you on Sunday. I can't wait. son'...

Geneva walks into the breakfast room now wearing her girdle and garter belt.
She needs Baba to help fasten her new silk stockings.
Baba tells Geneva to turn around and bend to the left a little...
Baba says if she had Geneva's curves she'd be dancing the foxtrot every night...

Shiner is coming in through the front door now with a bag of groceries...
He sees Geneva wearing only her girdle and says, 'I'm blind, Ma!'
He gives Geneva his, 'are you crazy' look— a look she has seen before...
'Phoebe is being nice enough to help me with my garter snaps,' Gene says.
'I can't see what I'm doing... back here... by my buttocks...'
Shiner laughs...

As Baba makes Geneva turn around, she tells Shiner that Pauline had a boy…
'Eight-twenty this morning,' she says. 'They named him Michael.'
'One more Moore to add to the Moores,' Shiner says. 'It's like magic.'

'This is just hard to do,' Baba says to Geneva. 'Why are you wearing a girdle?'
'I'd give my English soul to a Scot even, for a body like yours, girl.'
Geneva giggles now and says all the girls are wearing girdles these days…

SCENE 51
"CHEESE GOULASH AND FRENCH DRESSING" - SEPTEMBER 19, 1963

Today the tile workers finished remodeling the kitchen.
It took them three days to do it, and now my mother is finally happy.
All of Baba's white and black tile is gone—
Replaced with new tile of a light beige color.
The counters all look like something you might see in a soap commercial.
My mother says the kitchen looks a millions times better…
'Don't you think?'

Now Baba is being wheeled into the kitchen to see for herself…
My mother says she thinks the beige color is quite pretty—
'Plus, it offers a softer atmosphere and tone, don't you think?'
Baba looks at the new color, and angrily shakes her head…
'I can't stand it, Pauline,' Baba says. 'Worst thing I've ever seen.'
'That's exactly what I expected you to say, Phoebe.'
Now my mother is wheeling Baba out of the kitchen…
I can hear Baba whimpering as they go by.
My mother is smiling as she pushes Baba down the hallway…

It is dinner time now, and Baba has been wheeled into the breakfast room.
My father as usual stands and puts a white bib over Baba's lap.
Baba says, 'Thanks, son. Lord knows I need one of these now.'

My mother has made her first dinner in the newly remodeled kitchen.
She is serving my father's favorite tonight—
Cheese goulash with dinner rolls, and a green salad with french dressing.
Paul is seated next to me at the table as usual, but he is not in a good mood.
He isn't getting along with my mother.
They argue all the time about his lousy attitude, his grades, and his friends…

THE PINK OLEANDERS

Tonight they are fighting again, so he refuses to eat his salad.
My mother is telling him to grow up… 'to mature, or get out of the room!'
Baba is starting to cry now, as Paul gets up from the table and storms out…
'Grow up!' she yells, 'You need to do some serious thinking young man.'

Now Baba is starting to choke on her salad, as she spits it up on her bib…
"Fred, she's choking,' my mother says. 'Do something!'
'She's not choking. Pauline,' my father says.
'She's just upset with you two fighting again.'
Now he is wheeling his weeping mother out of the breakfast room…
My mother is smiling again as she eats her cheese goulash.

Finally there is peace in the house…
Baba is now resting peacefully in her bedroom after the family quarrel.
My mother is eating her second helping now, as she stares at my father…
'She's putting on, Fred.'
My father looks back at her, but as usual, says nothing at her remark…
Now there is a loud, god-awful cry coming from Baba's room…
It sounds like something you'd hear in a Vincent Price movie…
Both my parents get up and rush quickly to Baba's aid.
They find her on the floor beside the bed, writhing in pain…

Doctor Wilson has arrived.
My father does his taxes every year, so he owes my father a favor…
Presently, he's on the phone inside the breakfast room…

I am the eleven year old kid standing in the dark on the front yard lawn.
My mother told me to come out here when the doctor arrived.
All the house lights are on reminding me of a big sad Jack o'Lantern…

Here comes my father with Doctor Wilson.
They both look very worried.

My father says the doctor has called for an ambulance, and to stand back…

Finally the ambulance arrives and parks in front of the old Cox House.
Two men are taking a stretcher inside through the front door…
I am looking through the breakfast room windows to see what's going on…
Once again, Doctor Wilson is on the phone…

Here comes Baba now…
They are taking her on a stretcher to the ambulance…
The two men open the back door and slide her in.
They close the door now and are getting inside.
They silently drive up Hoover Street, stop at Beverly, and turn right.

SCENE 52
"WHAT HAVE YOU DONE TO ME?" - AUGUST 28, 1969

There I am, sitting worried on the back door porch.
I am filled with nauseating anxiety, and I can't stop biting my fingernails…
The thousands of stones in the middle of the driveway are silent.
They know nothing about what has happened between me and Teresa.
I seek private advice from anyone or anything, but to whom can I go…
To ask my question?

If only I had been able to control myself yesterday at her house.
But once we got on her green sofa…
Well… I had no idea how to stop what had already started between us…

Teresa was naked and I was on top of her, like James Bond in *Thunderball*,
Her skinny brown legs were spread apart, and there I was—
Dry-humping her like an amateur…
Except this time, I didn't stay dry.
Something took over my body; a sensation I never felt before.
On Teresa's stereo, the Iron Butterfly was playing *In A Gadda Da Vida*.
Doug Ingle's organ solo was playing in the background when it happened……

Next thing I knew, my semen was splattered on Teresa's hairy crotch…
'My god,' Teresa said, when she saw my stuff all over her—
'What have you done to me!'
Immediately we got up from the sofa, and she ran to the bathroom in a panic.
'I'm sorry, Teresa,' I kept saying to her through the closed bathroom door—
'I had no control.'
'My god,' she kept saying. 'It's all over me!'
'Can you get pregnant?' I asked, scared out of my mind.
'I don't know,' she said, very worried. 'Your stuff is even inside me!'

As I sit here on this porch, I can hear my father in the kitchen.
He is washing the dishes at the white sink.
I am so worried I cannot eat anything…
I need to go in there and ask if he would talk to me about my problem.
There is no way I can talk about this with my mother, or my brother even…
But I think my father would understand better, since he's a married guy.
I need to ask him if a girl can get pregnant if the guy doesn't cum inside her.
No. I can't ask my father that question…Am I crazy?
For sure he would tell my mother, and all hell will break loose…
I must sit like this for about three more weeks, than we will all know if she is…
I can't even say it…

THE PINK OLEANDERS

SCENE 53
"ETHEL WATERS PLAYING ON THE PHILCO" - SEPTEMBER 20, 1933

There's Harry in his garage at sunset…
He is working at his bench, fixing the broken handle of Baba's fry pan.
Through the open bathroom window he can hear music playing.
Shiner is playing a record on the Philco record player—
'Stormy Weather," sung by Ethel Waters…
Harry likes this song and decides to play the same record again later on…

Now Missus Morrison walks into the garage looking for Harry…
She says Phoebe needs her pan back so she can make supper now.
Missus Morrison is now looking at Harry's tools.
She says she thinks Harry's garage is 'well-organized and quite useful.'

Now she comes up to Harry and embraces him.
She whispers into his ear, thanking him for his financial help…
Harry says it is his pleasure, and that old Sydney Miners need to stick together.
Missus Morrison agrees that friends and family are all that matter.
'Times are hard for us,' she says. 'But you have made it easier, Harry.'
Harry says he needs to fetch his spade from behind the garage now…

He looks at Missus Morrison with a raised eye brow, and says,
'Care to join me?'
Now he walks into the orange sunset to the rear of his garage…
Inside the house, Shiner is playing an Ethel Waters record again—
This time it is "Dinah."

Dinah,
Is there anyone finer
In the state of Carolina?

If there is and you know her,
Show her!
Dinah,
With her Dixie eyes blazin',
How I love to sit and gaze in
To the eyes of Dinah Lee!

Now Missus Morrison follows Harry to the avocado tree behind the garage...

SCENE 54
"FLIRTING AT THE METROPOLE" - JUNE 18, 1960

Shiner and Geneva are sitting on the front room sofa talking with Baba.
The pink oleanders outside appear to be on fire as summer arrives.
Baba is seated in her gray rocking chair, listening sadly…

Geneva is telling her Mister Cox has died from a heart attack.
'He died yesterday, Phoebe,' Geneva says. 'Missus Cox said he went quickly.'
Baba says she's awfully sorry to hear the news. 'He was such a good soul.'
Shiner says they aren't having a funeral for him since he hated funerals.
'Maybe we can have something here,' Geneva says. 'But I don't know what…'
Shiner says he will talk it over with Missus Cox… 'Never mind, Geneva.'

It is noon now, and Baba is still sitting in her rocking chair…
Geneva is in the kitchen preparing sandwiches and tea for lunch.
She has the radio on as she pours black tea into three shiny cups.
The music playing reminds her of home in Nebraska…
It is the "Theme From A Summer Place" by Percy Faith…
Geneva is humming along now as she brings lunch into the breakfast room…
Baba likes the music as well, and tells Geneva to 'turn it up…'

She remembers back now to the old times as a working girl in Blackpool—
A nineteen year old barmaid working near the Promenade…
She recalls the music, the smell of frying fish, and the flirting at the Metropole.
There she learned to make the chasers and the fried Mackenflap.
There she met the wiry visitors from Liverpool and nearby Wigan…

One afternoon she had leave to climb the Tower as the wind blew hard.
A visitor from Wigan was there, standing by the fence, and scanning the view.
She recalls the wind was so strong, it blew the chap backwards a few feet…

That is when Phoebe Blinkhorn of Ince laughed at the chap.
'You need an anchor?'
The unknown chap smiled, and said he needed to 'gain more weight, I guess.'

She later noticed the skinny chap again, walking alone on the Promenade—
Looking hungry…

Now Geneva is bringing in Baba's steel wheelchair…
'I hate this 'orrible thing,' Baba says.
'I remember when I could run up the basement steps!'
Geneva says she knows, and that it's too bad Baba can't get around like before.
Now Geneva wheels Baba into the breakfast room…
'Here's your tea,' Geneva says. 'I hope you like this tuna fish, Phoebe.'
Baba now makes a face while Geneva walks back into the kitchen…

CHRISTMAS 1961 WITH DINT AND FRED ON THE SOFA; GENEVA AND SHINER IN THE BACK CENTER; BABA IS IN HER WHEELCHAIR, WHILE PAUL AND MIKE SIT IN THE FOREGROUND.

SCENE 55
"DID SHE SEE ANYONE?" - MARCH 22, 1964

The sun is setting behind me as I sit up here on this garage roof.
I am thinking about my dead grandparents...
I often wonder what death is like when it happens.
I wonder what grandpa went through when he died in the bathroom.
Did Baba feel any pain when she died, and did she see anything?... anyone?

Maybe it's like turning a TV set off...
Except, you are the TV set...

Today my parents drove out to Calvary Cemetery in Los Angeles.
They wanted to see Baba's new grave marker.
I decided to go because I like to visit graveyards.
When I walk amongst the dead I feel like I'm in a Hollywood horror movie.

On the way there, my mother complained, 'It took too long to get it set.'
'Six months is a ridiculously long time to have to wait for a tombstone.'
My father just chain-smoked his cigarettes like a nervous chimney.
'Fred,' she said, 'Take me to the cemetery office. I want to complain.'

Once we got to the gravesite, my mother finally stopped complaining.
Both graves were in an old area with hundreds of tall tombstones rising up.
Some of those stones had photographs of the dead person embedded into them.
But the gravestones for Baba and Grandpa were smaller, and flat on the ground.
And I noticed Grandpa's grave was sunken down more than Baba's new grave.

My father asked me if I wanted to say anything to them while we were there.
At first, I said no, but then, I thought about it, and decided I wanted to.
So we all stood facing the two graves and I said the Lord's Prayer.

After that, I spoke to Baba and told her the rose bushes out back are doing fine.
Then I turned to Grandpa and said nothing…
Instead, I knelt on one knee and tapped his gravestone three times…

Today was a cold overcast day in Los Angeles.
Clouds covered the skies all day long like a big gray quilt.
But now the sun has come out… just as it begins its slow, silent setting.
I think Grandpa's life was like this sunset.

THE END

THE AUTHOR IN 1964 AT THE GRAVES OF HIS GRANDPARENTS—
HARRY AND BABA — CALVARY CEMETERY, LOS ANGELES, CALIFORNIA

BABA IN 1961 WITH HER TWO GRANDSONS, PAUL AND THE AUTHOR.

ABOUT THE AUTHOR

BORN IN WHITTIER, CALIFORNIA IN 1952, Stark Hunter was an English teacher for 38 years before retiring from the classroom in 2017. He has written and published 12 books, which are available on Amazon.com and Barnes & Noble.com: *In A Gadda Da Vida*, a novel, published in 2002, *Carnivorous Avenues*, a poetry volume published in 2004, *Flies*, a short novel published in 2005, *Private Diaries*, a satire published in 2006, *Voices From Clark Cemetery*, a poetry volume published in 2013, *Cocktails For the Soul*, a poetry anthology published in 2013, *Voices From Mt. Olive Cemetery*, a poetry volume published in 2018, *Digested by the Dust*, another poetry anthology, published in 2018, Scenes From the Cerebellum, published in 2019, Monster Trees, published in 2020, White Sidewalks in 2021, and Covid Gardens in 2021.

Hunter's work has also been published by the Lothlorien Poetry Journal and SpillWords Press in 2021.

His poetry was included in the following Poetry Anthologies: Stars In Our Hearts, Visions, published 2012 (World Poetry Movement); In My Lifetime, Chronicles, published 2013 (Eber and Wein Publishing); PS: It's Poetry, An Anthology Of Eclectic Contemporary Poems Written By Poets From Around the Globe, published 2020 (PoetrySoup.Com).

Four of the author's poems were read on Diverse TV with host, Alexandro Botelho, for his program, "Live Writings On The Wall" in 2021. The author has also been a guest on Chat and Spin Radio from the UK, and on the GMAP Broadcast Network with Pastor Kevin Strawder in 2021.

Fourteen of Mr. Hunter's poems from *Voices From Clark Cemetery* were adopted and set to music by Dr. George Mabry, composer and former conductor of the Nashville Symphony Chorus, for his work, *Voices*, a musical drama which was performed at Austin Peay State University in Clarksville, Tennessee in 2015.

Mr. Hunter's poetry works can be perused at poetrysoup.com. and allpoetry.com.

Mr. Hunter is married with two daughters, a granddaughter, and resides in Chino Hills, California.

www.ingramcontent.com/pod-product-compliance
Lightning Source LLC
Chambersburg PA
CBHW020935090426
42736CB00010B/1150